Take Pride

How to build organisational success through people

Sheila Parry

Unbound

This edition first published in 2018

Unbound
6th Floor Mutual House, 70 Conduit Street, London W1S 2GF

www.unbound.com

Text Design by PDQ

A CIP record for this book is available from the British Library

ISBN 978-1-78352-634-5 (trade pbk)
ISBN 978-1-78352-636-9 (ebook)
ISBN 978-1-78352-635-2 (limited edition)

Printed in Great Britain by CPI Group (UK)

To Robyn, David and Mark,
and the next generation of people at work

Dear Reader,

The book you are holding came about in a rather different way to most others. It was funded directly by readers through a new website: Unbound. Unbound is the creation of three writers. We started the company because we believed there had to be a better deal for both writers and readers. On the Unbound website, authors share the ideas for the books they want to write directly with readers. If enough of you support the book by pledging for it in advance, we produce a beautifully bound special subscribers' edition and distribute a regular edition and ebook wherever books are sold, in shops and online.

This new way of publishing is actually a very old idea (Samuel Johnson funded his dictionary this way). We're just using the internet to build each writer a network of patrons. At the back of this book, you'll find the names of all the people who made it happen.

Publishing in this way means readers are no longer just passive consumers of the books they buy, and authors are free to write the books they really want. They get a much fairer return too – half the profits their books generate, rather than a tiny percentage of the cover price.

If you're not yet a subscriber, we hope that you'll want to join our publishing revolution and have your name listed in one of our books in the future. To get you started, here is a £5 discount on your first pledge. Just visit unbound.com, make your pledge and type **take5** in the promo code box when you check out.

Thank you for your support,

Dan, Justin and John
Founders, Unbound

Contents

Introduction:
The PRIDE Concept

Ask anyone you know what makes them feel proud. Guaranteed, their eyes will light up, they will express something with passion and you will witness a surge of emotion. It's a great question to ask, because it brings out a positive expression of warmth that makes people feel good about themselves or others. Talking about people or occasions that evoke pride reinforces positivity and a sense of achievement. Moments of pride make for strong, potentially bonding memories that people want to share with others.

Take Pride will show you how to create those positive emotions in the workplace, for yourself and for people who work for you.

There is a compelling business case for pride at work – pride in oneself and in one's organisation leads to better personal and collective performance. People with pride will make more effort, make better decisions, forge better relationships with their customers, and exert more positive influence on their colleagues. They will also take more care of their own and their organisation's reputation. People with pride are generally happier and healthier. They are more confident in their own abilities, are more fulfilled, and are less likely to suffer from stress.

Take Pride is for leaders and influencers who want work to be a great place for the majority, not the minority, and who are looking for a fresh approach to make it happen.

This book sets out the PRIDE business model, which through generating Purpose, Reputation, Integrity, Direction and Energy at work will create the environment where people respect each other, understand and share goals, want to contribute and know that they are valued. In building personal and professional pride, the model will drive performance and make people and the organisations they work for more successful.

The PRIDE approach has wider consequences for our economic performance. The need for fulfilling work is universal, and yet in the UK only one in three people is actively engaged in what they do. More than that, another one in four is actively disengaged, a trend that can only deplete national productivity and output. The remaining millions of people who lean neither one way nor the other represent a mass of potential energy and productive effort that is currently going to waste. While most organisations talk about the importance of employee motivation, few of them adopt clear strategies to achieve it. This picture is not unique to the UK.

This book explores what makes us feel pride, why it matters, and how to create the conditions in the workplace that make people proud of who they are and what they do. Part philosophy, part methodology, it has the potential to move people management in the workplace from poor to average, and then from average to a good performance on a massive scale.

Good job, bad job. Know the difference

I have worked with some of the world's largest companies and best-known brands, helping them achieve greater engagement, performance and success through their people. I have worked with charismatic leaders and inclusive managers who have created energetic and positive cultures in the workplace. As an employer myself, I have applied best practice in my own communications agency, and I have first-hand experience of building a positive culture, where people are proud to work.

On other occasions, however, I have observed appalling behaviour by people in positions of responsibility, who have displayed bad manners, bad management or just sheer incompetence. I have seen toxic relationships, where people have lost respect and trust in their employers and are afraid to speak their minds.

I also know what it is like to hate my job. As a school-leaver, I spent a miserable few months working for a renowned television documentary producer who was brilliant, but a bully. I was the most junior person in the company – the one who answered phones, made coffee, met guests and ran all the errands. I had been thrilled to get the job, but my early excitement was short-lived. After a few weeks of verbal abuse from the producer, I decided that the job just wasn't worth the humiliation. I was just a runner, so I ran. As I did so, I vowed that work was too important to me to accept second-best again. If I was going to feel good about work and do something well, I had to be in a place where I was valued. And I would never stay in a job where I was unhappy.

Forty years on, I know what it feels like to love my job and be proud of what I do, and I am passionate about helping other people feel the same. I have made it my business to 'make work better', not just for me but for others.

Two principles, five factors

The PRIDE model is built on five factors. Before explaining them, I want to introduce the two core principles that anchor the PRIDE approach.

Principle #1: Adopt a dual perspective

Our daily experience of work is influenced by multiple factors from the macro (broad economic trends and market forces) to the micro (our bosses' personality and our colleagues' enthusiasm). Throw in, for good measure, the mood we wake up in, the relationships we have at home, and whether we feel we have any choices in life. All this counts.

Over my years at work, I've become more and more convinced that wherever we work, whatever our brands stand for, however good our ideas or products, for anything to have any meaning or make real impact you need to find the right people. In every company, every workplace I have known, it is the individual who makes things happen. I challenge any business leader, any consultant, to look at the most complex challenges they have faced, the most complex structures they have managed, and not acknowledge the part played by particular, influential individuals.

Every large company comprises multiple functions and departments, smaller networks or groups of people working in shifts, in teams or alone. Whatever the workplace, how people behave is the difference between a good and a bad experience there. 'People make the difference' is not an empty expression.

Recognising the power of the individual, *this book adopts a unique dual perspective on the world of work* – through the lens of the organisation and through those of individual employees. Easy in theory, in practice this dual perspective is a challenge to maintain. It requires a step-change from established management thinking to both knowing and caring what employees are thinking.

Principle #2: Bring your whole brain to work

If you want to build pride in your organisation and to see colleagues taking pride in their roles, you need to appeal to people's rational and emotional triggers. Being successful and building successful organisations is hard work. It takes guts and heart, and you have to engage your brain – every bit of it.

As a creative communicator, I have some strong right-brain tendencies. But to make good in the world of business I have had to develop the left side of my brain – my logical, numerical and fact-based skills. The PRIDE model will resonate with those in Communications and HR because they should already be tuned in to the motivations of people at work and have the emotional intelligence to see how it might apply to their own organisation. But to play their full part, they need to understand their organisation's business goals as well. They need to connect the personal to the strategic, the individual to the collective, and to convince the leadership of the model's merits. To be effective, you not only have to use the language of leadership, you have to start thinking like leaders as well.

On the other hand, when it comes to leadership, people and organisations are successful when they are led by a well-rounded team. *Technical ability and intelligence alone do not make a leader; you need to have sensitivity and emotional intelligence as well.* Emotional intelligence means being aware of how you and other people are feeling as well as behaving – working out the why, as well as the what. It displays itself in active listening, empathy, and the ability to adjust your behaviour to suit the needs of others. The most effective organisations recognise the need for softer skills and create the opportunities for leaders to develop their empathy. This book will give logical thinkers a new way of thinking about human interactions in the workplace.

People and their performance will flourish when leaders and influencers pay attention to both evidence and intuition, where good relationships are viewed as an integral part of leadership responsibility, and good behaviour is rewarded alongside good results.

Witnessing the great results achieved when CEOs and strategic HR and Communications people work hand in hand was a catalyst for me to create the PRIDE model, which steps away from the single-functional, specialist communications approach to look at the business environment as a whole.

The PRIDE model

What is it that drives people's motivation and commitment to their work? What gets them up in the morning? What keeps them on track? What really makes them tick? A key driver is pride – in their company, in their brand and in their role.

The PRIDE model identifies five common factors that build pride at work. This book explains what these factors are, why they matter, what they look like up close, and how they can be achieved.

Factor #1: Purpose

At the beginning, middle and end of the PRIDE approach, **purpose** defines a company's raison d'être. Purpose is deeply meaningful, proudly shared and readily discussed. It drives sustainable and emotional commitment from employees and strengthens commercial relationships.

Factor #2: Reputation

A company's **reputation** is usually a key motivation for potential employees and the yardstick of a company's commercial value in the world. It can be measured, promoted and impacted by numerous factors, and can affect financial performance across a range of dimensions from brand value to share price.

Factor #3: Integrity

I define this factor as a company's 'inner truth'. **Integrity** is the evidence of whether the reputation is signalled in the day-to-day experience of its key stakeholders, and reflected in the policies and practices of the organisation, across such processes and events as employee induction, management incentive schemes, customer opinion or communications.

Factor #4: Direction

Direction is a statement of a company's future focus – its strategy for growth and its goals. Employees want to know what the company's next step will be, how they fit in with it, how they will develop, and what personal benefit they will gain from it.

Factor #5: Energy

To reach its direction, a company has to maintain its momentum. **Energy** comes from inside and outside sources and builds the physical and emotional stamina that will achieve sustainability for a company and its brand.

Purpose, Reputation, Integrity, Direction, Energy – each plays its part in an ethos that fosters individual and collective performance. Each component counts in its own right, but together they can have tremendous impact on the relationship employees have with their organisation and their brand.

In chapters 1 to 5 I explore each factor, and give examples of how Communications and HR people can help establish it within an organisation's culture. In the sixth and final chapter I present a diagnostic and methodology to measure and improve pride in your organisation, enabling you and your employees to reach their goals and achieve greater success in the future.

What are the factors that drive PRIDE?

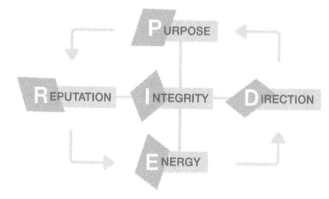

1
Purpose

What is Purpose?

Broadly, purpose is a clear definition of the positive impact that your organisation makes on society. It is more than the achievement of a revenue value or sales figure, greater than a single brand proposition, or the specification of your products or services. It reaches beyond the singular, direct experience of your customers, your employees or your shareholders. It concerns the contribution your organisation makes to the world, above and beyond the immediate and demanding metrics that make up your strategic plan.

Organisations with a compelling and clearly articulated purpose are more successful in attracting and retaining staff. They are proven to have greater relationships with their customers, deliver greater shareholder value, and they outperform their competitors in terms of performance, productivity, longevity and culture.[1]

As with every other aspect of the PRIDE model, purpose also has a strong personal dimension. People have emotions, aspirations and dreams. Their sense of purpose is defined by their personal desires and wishes, by their needs and ambitions, at different times in different ways. People will feel a sense of purpose inside and outside their role at work, and the emphasis may change, depending on where they are in their lives, and their feelings of responsibility for themselves or others.

A statement of organisational purpose bestows importance and significance on the everyday activities that occupy people at work. But it has to be authentic. Few people get up in the morning to fulfil a mission to save the world or to implement a strategy. They do so because someone needs them to do something and they are driven to fulfil a role. Purpose feeds into that drive and creates a positive energy, so that – at best – employees come to work not only because they are being paid, but also because the organisation's purpose appeals to their higher values and emotions, and they are committed to their role within it.

Herein lies the business case. When people can fulfil their own ambitions and at the same time identify with and share a sense of purpose with the organisation that employs them, they are more motivated, more resourceful, and exert more effort in their roles. People with purpose are happier, healthier, and have a high level of self-esteem.

In this chapter we will look at how different organisations define purpose, how they then deliver it in their specific organisation, and how that is played out and taken on by the people who work for them.

Finding Purpose

For some organisations, purpose to society (also referred to as social purpose) has been there from the start; it is their raison d'être. It has been defined, articulated, and provides an essential guiding vision for all to see. Think public sector, foundations, charities; think healthcare and educational bodies. Their core service offering and daily activity directly indicate their purpose. Customers, beneficiaries, employees and other stakeholders are most likely to be involved in the organisation precisely because of its commitment to society, and thus they share common motivations and values. For these companies, purpose is intrinsic.

For others, social purpose has been expressed as a distinct motivation underpinning the core activity but not defining it. The products and services of the organisation are not unique, but the way they are produced, or the way the organisation conducts itself, is. An example here is The Body Shop, whose founder, Anita Roddick, was an entrepreneur trying to make a living, who decided on the skincare and cosmetics sector, but wanted also to prove that business could be a force for social and environmental good. Roddick declared this motivation with her employees from day one, and expected them to reflect it. She developed a social purpose for The Body Shop that spelled itself out not only in what the company did (the products it created) but also in the way it operated (championing fair trade in the cosmetics supply chain) and the causes it supported. Its social purpose went beyond the provision of cosmetics and beyond its time as an independently owned manufacturer, surviving intact forty years on, ten years after the founder's death and its acquisition by the Brazilian ethical company Natura.

In a similar vein, the challenger clothing brand Gandys, established in 2014, is proving that fashion can be a force for good. The company was founded by the brothers Rob and Paul Forkan, as a vehicle to support Orphans for Orphans, a foundation that helps children affected by the 2004 tsunami, where they too lost their parents. Passionate travellers and volunteers, they opened their first children's home in Sri Lanka in 2014 and their first store in London in 2016, and their goal is to continue to grow on both dimensions. Their vision is to provide more safe facilities for disadvantaged children and their communities, and at the same time create more products, inspired by a sense of adventure. They signal the purpose of their brand actively online and instore, and commit 10 per cent of their profits to the foundation.

For many perfectly reputable organisations, an articulation of social purpose can take longer to emerge. Most commercial businesses are founded to meet a market need or fill a market gap, and their organisational purpose is to fill that gap, make money for their shareholders and provide jobs for their employees. Often, with maturity, with scale and with influence, when initial organisational goals have been fulfilled or proved, leaders of these organisations may begin to seek and realise deeper meaning and relevance in what they are doing. Perceiving the power they possess, or their desire to influence society, they begin to envision a social or 'higher' purpose that is borne out by their success and a real contribution to society. Procter & Gamble (P&G), Unilever and Virgin are three such examples. All of them were established and grown by visionary entrepreneurs with a social conscience, who stayed true to their organisational purpose but at the same time invested time and resources into undertaking some broader responsibility to society as well.

For others, a statement of purpose has emerged under more negative pressures, perhaps when organisations have been under threat or failing, and are forced to reassess and reinvent themselves in response to a change in market conditions. They may want to differentiate themselves in a competitive market by adopting a higher purpose, or they may need to redefine their organisational purpose to regain support from investors or customers, or even to survive a crisis.

For many organisations, however, purpose, as a way of providing relevance and meaning, is uncharted territory. Products are made, services provided, transactions done. But purpose has no place on the map, it is not articulated, and its benefits as yet go unexplored.

In your role at work, you are not necessarily responsible for all that has gone before, let alone all that is likely to happen in the future. But wherever you are in your own or your organisation's story, you can find moments or opportunities to make an impact. If you are a leader or an influencer of an organisation without a clear declaration of purpose, addressing this matter offers one such opportunity, as the topic is gaining ground as a significant factor influencing stakeholder engagement with your brand.[2]

Why now?

There are several reasons for this. The emergence of purpose as a driving concept for organisations is in part a consequence of the mass consumerism of the twentieth century, and has been greatly accelerated in the turmoil following the 2008–9 recession. But without doubt it has been further strengthened by the new wave of informed and discerning Gen Ys, or millennials* entering the workforce in its wake. Let's look at those factors in turn.

Kickback from crises

A whistle-stop tour through the trending topics of our recent industrialised past sees too many companies, from the 1950s to the present day, steeped in a rigid focus on capital gain, a bias towards fast return on investment and short-term thinking. For listed companies, delivering quarterly results to the capital markets and satisfying shareholders still dominates business culture, and this has launched waves of strategic programmes to deliver maximised resources and profitability, sometimes at the expense of higher values and culture. Mergers and acquisitions in the richest business sectors such as fast-moving consumer goods (FMCG), finance, pharmaceuticals and automotive, have created giants, some of which have been a force for good, while others have systematically abused their position of power.

Customers increasingly got a look-in. As the baby boomers joined the workforce in the 1970s and 1980s, schools of market-led theory emerged, preaching the desires of customer personas and the need for customer-centricity, the customer journey and the concept of a customer-service culture. The customer had new money so the customer was king. By the end of the twentieth century, rapid technological advance had created more new markets, new sectors, a new way of life that the commercial world still strives to satisfy. Marketing experts tell us that we, the consumers, now get to influence the brands we buy, have more choice and a more powerful voice than ever before, and that this is still a growing trend. As a result, brands not only sell products, they also have to establish meaningful relationships with consumers.

---

* Definitions of Gen Ys and millennials vary, but generally refer to those born between the early 1980s and late 1990s, as children of baby boomers, and maturing into adult life in the early twenty-first century.

At the same time, through a century of galloping materialism, the problems we materialists were creating began to be too big for any one government or public body to solve. While it has meant wealth for the few, we are more and more aware of the polarisation of economies and diminishing global resources. The democratisation of our relationships with brands, it seems, has changed not only the way we communicate, but also the way we regard responsibility. If we are all in this together, we have to adopt a broader view of our accountabilities, including protecting the planet for future generations.

Faced with the social and environmental impact of what capitalism has created, governments and regulators looked at who was responsible and began by creating triple bottom-line reporting, demanding some tangible efforts both from individuals and from businesses to devise environmentally robust solutions that limit the damage of all that production and consumption. In the last generation, social responsibility for people, community and the environment has gained tremendous ground across all sectors, as many established and new companies have been variously spurred on by public opinion and NGO-led socially sustainable policies. The year 2016 saw the establishment of the Global Commission on Business and Sustainable Development, now chaired by former UN Deputy Secretary General Lord Mark Malloch-Brown and supported by leaders from global businesses including Unilever, Ericsson, Merck, Safaricom and Edelman. Alongside its commitment to drive global adoption of a set of strategic sustainable development goals, the Commission also aims to show how businesses can align profitability with social purpose.[3]

Yet, for all the positive motivations to improve society and the declarations issued by the best of these private–public partnerships, there are other circumstantial motivations at play. In the developed economies, and particularly in the UK, our current mood, as consumers and workers, has been dampened by a decade of grievous crises. The collapse of the financial markets, the consequences of toxic debt, and a stagnation or drop in net income among all but the richest in our society, caused a widescale crisis of confidence in many established institutions across the developed world.

Individual business scandals from Enron and Exxon to Tesco and Volkswagen are symptomatic of an age that had grown obsessed by financial gain and riddled with corporate greed. Big names – and a lot of them – fell victims to the recession and failed by their own standards of financial success; others fell by their own systemic mismanagement and corruption. All of this has caused a massive backlash among ordinary people and their representatives, who have forced changes in the way business is run.

Ten years on since the US housing market's bubble burst, the US, UK and other markets in Europe are beginning to declare a recovery, but consumer mistrust will prevent a return to old ways. In fact commentators are saying there is 'a new normal' in business practice, and the business landscape has changed for ever. Now, businesses face much more scrutiny on governance, regulation and compliance controls, and their activity is more openly assessed by customers, shareholders and employees.

Traditional and social media have turned up the volume on corporate greed, and large corporations have been challenged to re-examine their principles and practices. Continuing investigations into creative corporation tax management (aka tax avoidance) at Starbucks, Amazon and Google – companies otherwise frequently cited as the business success stories of our generation – only redouble the urgent call for businesses to give account of their value to society.

Business has not been the only culprit in the last decade and the public sector has also failed the public in many damaging cases. The MPs' expenses scandal of 2009 in the UK was disastrous for public confidence in the integrity of Parliament, and led to demand for the widespread release of information in the public interest. Open government, spearheaded and delivered by founders of the Open Data Institute in the UK, is just one significant outcome in the unstoppable pressure for greater transparency and accountability in the way the public sector works.

Media scandals such as the phone-hacking by News International, and the apparent cover-up by the BBC of allegations of child abuse by Jimmy Savile, added further layers of public disillusion in the

UK, and by 2015 most commentators agreed that trust in almost every sector of the UK establishment had reached record lows. One month before the 2015 General Election, a UK survey showed that government, politicians and tabloid newspapers were the three least trusted entities of society, below bankers and trade unions.[4]

In the last few years, both the public and private sectors have been forced to assess their standing with their stakeholders and seek ways to retrieve their reputations. They have revisited their mission statements, changed their tone and embraced some new perspectives. The redefinition of meaning, the reassertion of values, and a new focus on communicating a social purpose has not come about solely because of a spontaneous surge of corporate conscience. Rather, these actions have an additional commercial motivation, in that they can be instrumental in rebuilding public confidence.

About the millennials

Has any previous generation been so frequently analysed as the millennials? Historians and futurologists, economists and social anthropologists, marketers and the media industry all have a take on the new wave born with technology. And just about anyone with a blog has an insight to offer. There is a huge mass of data on how they view the world, what their moral compass is, how they think, act and, of course, communicate on just about every subject on the planet, and there are just as many opinions. In the context of purpose at work, a few stand out for scrutiny.

First comes Lynda Gratton's *The Shift: The Future of Work Is Already Here*,[5] recommended to me in 2012 by my long-established client Dean Capon, then at Roche Pharma. Gratton proposes generational demographics as one of the five global forces that are most impacting the future of work (the others are technology, globalisation, society and energy). Supported by her research paper *The Reflexive Generation: Young Professionals' Perspectives on Work, Career and Gender*,[6] she points to millennials' self-reliance and sense of responsibility, a desire for learning and personal development, their constant reappraisal of their own role in society, and determination not to repeat the mistakes of their parents and strive for better work–life balance. This plays to a working life of multiple employers or careers, a need for regular feedback and promotion, encouragement to develop transferable skills, and the desire for more purposeful work. As people begin to think more deeply about themselves, they will work out what matters to them, in a way that may challenge their employers.

Regular studies by global management consultants PwC (PricewaterhouseCoopers) and Deloitte bear out these predictions and throw up a few more insights into millennials in the workplace.[7] Their familiarity with and command of technology is probably the most common theme of all. It has given them instant access to information, services and people all their lives, and they now want to see this matched in their workplace. Immediacy leads to a desire for more feedback, faster career progression and greater flexibility, scrapping the draconian, slow-moving hierarchies that reward age and experience over current value and contribution.

Research also points to greater emphasis on personal needs, informed opinions on work–life balance, a desire for meaningful flexibility at work, and recognition of personal impact. Studies claim that millennials are just as interested in how a business develops its people and its contribution to society as they are in its products and profits, and are sending a signal to leaders to revisit the definition of business. How far these differences are simply a feature of any younger generation, of youth, rather than unique to Gen Ys, is still open to debate.

From my own experience of living and working with millennials, I would point to a couple of other vital traits. First, one of the impacts technology has had is that they have all had greater exposure – at least by way of a screen – to the world's more ugly problems. War, poverty, inequality, racism, health and social issues, government and business corruption – there is nothing they have not seen or heard of, or cannot find online. This means they have access to more knowledge of and views on a wide range of issues. I also believe they have a more rigorous sense of fairness and have developed a greater understanding not only of what may be possible but also of their own ability to make a difference.

Perhaps due to the recent collapse of trust in government, they also prefer to take their lives into their own hands, more so than any generation before them. According to Pamela Hartigan, co-author of *The Power of Unreasonable People: How Social Entrepreneurs Create Markets That Change the World*,[8] today's young idealists differ from their predecessors:

> In the 1960s and 1970s, politics was the way we thought of changing the world. But young people today believe that change is going to be brought about by business and market discipline. And so they seek to set up enterprises, not to pad their pockets, but to transform what is broken in our societies in a long-lasting way.

Youthful optimism is not unique, but millennials have also grown up having access to more people, including friends and influencers, outside their own immediate family and social groups. Mostly, they have developed an ability to judge those influences, and they find movements of people who want to do something about some of the world's problems. They also have greater confidence to express themselves, and wider spheres of influence in their own right. Most of their communication is online, of course, but that is a powerful medium that simply wasn't available to previous generations.

While millennials may add to the pressure on business to act responsibly, seeking purpose is a universal human motivation, irrespective of age. I believe it is human nature to yearn to live and be free, to develop skills and to use them, to create and nurture relationships, to build families and communities that live in harmony. To achieve something that has wider impact than our own survival or our own personal comfort is, some believe, the greatest human goal. In spite of the rise in corporate interest in purpose in the workplace, businesses continue to look at the issue from the organisation's point of view, and these fundamentals of individual purpose remain woefully unexplored.

People seek purpose, in different manifestations, all their lives. A meaningful role at work can provide a great sense of purpose, and it is up to the creators and leaders of organisations to create the right framework to support this. But work is just one aspect of purpose, and not necessarily the most important. It does not have to be its sole provider, and arguably it should not be. From my own perspective, work contributes hugely to a sense of purpose; people want to feel they are achieving something. What matters most is that two perspectives – that of the organisation and that of the individual – are always in sight. Harmony prevails when the organisational purpose established at work is in tune with the individual's.

Perhaps we give more airtime to purpose when we are young, or perhaps, like the corporates, we revisit it at times of crisis when something forces us to reassess our actions or our values. But finding and following our own sense of self-worth is by no means the privilege of millennials. As Adam Grant, business psychologist and author of *Give and Take*,[9] asserts, the argument is clear:

> Whether we're Boomers, Gen Xers, or millennials, we're searching for interesting, meaningful jobs that challenge and stretch us. For jobs that allow us to support our lives and families outside work, earn respect and form significant relationships, and make a difference in the lives of others.

My view is that when it comes to aligning personal ambitions with those of an organisation, millennials are showing the self-confidence to demand it, and have the connectivity that will empower them to do so. They have created a groundswell of opinion. Now is the time for businesses and organisations to work out how to give them what we all want, and have wanted for generations.

Bringing Purpose into the mainstream

Let's be clear about putting purpose on your organisation's agenda. This move really need not be a threat. It does not rule out your existing organisational goals, and will not harm your power to make a profit. Finding and promoting purpose is an enriching and unifying dimension that can add sustainable value to your organisation. The point is to make it meaningful and make it real.

In the wake of the 2008–9 economic crisis, there was a flurry of commentators examining how to approach recovery and do things differently. In 2010 in his book *Reinventing Management*,[10] London Business School professor Julian Birkinshaw claimed that the organisations that had failed so spectacularly (in this case, Lehman Brothers) had demonstrated 'a deeply flawed approach to management that encouraged bankers to pursue opportunities without regard for their long-term consequences, and to put their own interests ahead of those of their employers and their shareholders'. The company, he said, lacked any higher purpose and focused on financial reward at the expense of all else; it cared nothing for teamwork, institution-building or loyalty. It was time to reconnect the visionaries with the workers and to re-instil shared values. Two years later, in *Culture Shock*,[11] claiming that business was broken, Will McInnes put forward a more impassioned manifesto to appeal for an entirely new system for business that was ethical, empowering and ultimately more democratic. Putting meaning and purpose back on the agenda was the beginning, but it had to be supported by new systems of transparency and financial fairness. While I believe that McInnes's approach is good for the brave and great for start-up, challenger brands, there are many, more traditional, businesses that need a more evolutionary approach.

Current members of the enterprise 'establishment' have since offered a rather different and probably more attractive motivation for finding organisation purpose: the argument that purpose does not deliver only social good, but profit too. In his 2012 book *Grow*,[12] global brand guru Jim Stengel has shown how fifty of the highest-performing companies in the world harnessed the power of higher ideals (akin to social purpose) not only to mark themselves out from their competitors but also to outdo them. In his TED talk[†] on the subject, Stengel speaks very personally about the catalyst for his own pursuit of higher values, and while this

---

† TED (Technology, Education and Design) is a non-profit organisation dedicated to 'sharing ideas and sparking conversations that will change the world'.

does him credit, I believe that the real appeal of his argument does not lie in purpose per se, but in its correlation with commercial performance. Just like earlier research that led to Jim Collins's best-selling business book *Good to Great*,[13] that correlation is much more compelling to the guardians of capitalist enterprise, for whom the potential clash between purpose and profit is still a concern.

Both Collins and Stengel had the benefit of knowing the inside story of a truly lasting and purposeful brand, Procter & Gamble (P&G). Collins wrote about it in his earlier work *Built to Last*,[14] citing it as a truly visionary company, and Stengel spent twenty-five years there in the role of Head of Global Brand. The founders of P&G were candle- and soap-makers, and they believed in supplying goods of superior quality and value, introducing 'Honest Grade, Honest Weight', their first business ethics promise to their customers in 1887. They also established an impressive heritage of creating community benefit, building hospitals, colleges and schools in Cincinnati since the nineteenth century. A century before most companies embarked on corporate social responsibility (CSR) programmes, in 1915 P&G founders' families spearheaded the first coordinated campaign on behalf of charities in Cincinnati, called The United Way. P&G documented their purpose and values as early as 1985, stating: 'Our purpose unifies us in a common cause and growth strategy of improving more consumers' lives in small but meaningful ways each day.'[15]

In the FMCG market, Anglo-Dutch rival Unilever had similar roots in soap-making with a social purpose. Back in 1888, William Hesketh Lever, the founder of what is now Unilever, created Port Sunlight in the north-west of England to provide housing, education and health services to workers in his soap factory. The village housed more than three thousand people and remained in the company's hands until the 1980s, when individual properties were sold. Over the last century, Unilever has extended its social influence to improving people's lives, supporting causes in many markets where it operates, and driving programmes to pipe clean water and encourage personal hygiene. Evocative of its 1926 Clean Hands Campaign in the UK, the Unilever brand Lifebuoy launched the world's largest hygiene-promotion programme with Oxfam and UNICEF in 2010, which aims to change the hand-washing behaviours of a billion people by 2020. Lifebuoy hand wash, now marketing in India and Indonesia, has a property that turns it from white to green in ten seconds, the time it takes to protect against 99.9 per cent of germs. Children wait for the soap to change colour before rinsing their hands.

Unilever is possibly the best-known current example of a purpose-led corporation, epitomised in its CEO Paul Polman, who joined the company in 2009 after twenty-seven years at P&G. Polman has been a key business figure in sustainability and climate change for years, but since joining Unilever has broadened his commentary on the urgent corporate responsibility to include issues such as global unemployment, social cohesion and food security. He has stated often that a lack of any robust global governance makes it imperative for businesses to intervene in the challenges facing the world 'because it is not clear who will step in otherwise'. He also speaks of the responsibility on corporates to shift investor perspectives towards a longer-term view: 'We are often trapped in short-termism and other things. There are still significant numbers of investors looking for the biggest possible short-term returns who do not care too much how companies achieve their dividends.'[16] Within Unilever he has stopped reporting quarterly results, so as to encourage shareholders and market analysts to adjust their views accordingly.

Reviewing the history of these two global giants, it is obvious that they have poured physical assets and emotional commitment into delivering a social purpose beyond their commercial performance, and this matters hugely in their stakeholder engagement. Through purpose, they engage with their customers beyond the bounds of a transactional exchange; they attract great talent across all disciplines, as they are seen to offer opportunities not only to learn but to contribute; they bring new products to new markets; and they reinvest in the planet's future resources.

Equally, none of their efforts in conducting a purpose-led strategy have detracted from the quest for their own commercial and operational excellence. They have built their organisations on core strengths of process engineering, product innovation, iconic branding and advertising, constantly investing in market research and customer insight. These are all features that make them successful businesses and attractive employers. They have shown that purpose is key not only to maintaining reputations but also to recruiting and keeping talent in the future. According to Unilever, it is the third most sought-after employer globally on LinkedIn, with half of graduate entrants citing the company's ethical policies and purpose as the primary reason for wanting to join. In addition, more than 76 per cent of all Unilever employees feel that their role at work helps to deliver the global sustainability agenda.

Early adopters like P&G and Unilever have already proved the commercial, reputational and societal benefits that derive from building businesses with purpose. They have put their higher, or social, purpose at the heart of their business model, in step with achieving an outstanding reputation in all areas. They have cracked the profit–purpose challenge, and for that applause is due. The boldest and brightest of future companies are already following their lead because they recognise that a statement of social purpose can provide an engine to drive the renaissance of institutional trust, as it serves both to set higher moral standards for governance and at the same time to restore credibility with a public now cynical and bruised.

According to the 2016 Edelman Trust Barometer, if corporates seek to satisfy the public, the upward trend will definitely continue.

> Certainly, business leaders must focus on strong financial performance, but increasingly, people correlate societal action with trust in business. Eight in 10 respondents believe that a company can take specific actions that both increase profits and improve the economic and social conditions in the community where it operates. And the same number say it's the responsibility of business to lead to solve societal problems – that's a 6% increase from just a year ago.

The last decade has seen a palpable shift in the tensions between profit and purpose, in which some players claim the moral high ground and portray themselves as a new type of business for a new type of stakeholder. While higher ideals and ethics are laudable, I believe it is the proven commercial benefit, such as market or brand differentiation, that will bring purpose into the mainstream. The challenge will arise from the way it is done.

Senior leaders and influencers in business confirm this view. The most recent research from *Harvard Business Review* in collaboration with global consultancy firm Ernst & Young (now branded as EY)[17] found that almost 100 per cent of the 474 board-level executives surveyed believed that purpose was important, yet admitted not knowing how to practise it.

The report sets out how executives view the power of purpose to transform their organisations, and assesses the pros and cons of embedding it within their companies. Of the executives surveyed, 89 per cent said that a strong sense of collective purpose drives employee satisfaction, while 84 per cent said it can affect an organisation's ability to transform, and 80 per cent said it helps increase customer loyalty. However, less than half of the executives surveyed said that their organisations had a strong sense of purpose, or had a strategic programme in mind to pursue it.

This opens the door to advocates of the PRIDE model. Purpose is not only for the millennials, or for the Unilevers of this world. Purpose can belong to everyone. Future-focused people need to get this on the organisational agenda and demonstrate the hugely positive impact it has on the way stakeholders regard and respect their organisation. Next we will look at how it can happen.

The organisation is the people

One of the core principles of the PRIDE model is that it sets up a view of work through the dual lenses of the organisation and of its people. To make PRIDE work, you will need to explore the relationships that people have with their organisation, and to think about the impact of an individual's words and actions on the shared experience in the workplace.

Company culture expresses prevailing sets of individual behaviours. It starts with the founder and founding associates, the decisions they make and the businesses they partner with, but as the company grows, other individuals make a conscious decision to sign up and adhere to organisational goals and norms.

In order for the deal between employer and employee to work, there needs to be a continuous circle of harmony between the beliefs, aspirations and behaviours of the collective organisation and those of the individual. Whatever the size of your organisation, the true measure of its reputation and its reality, its past, its present and its future, comes from people.

For that reason, throughout the PRIDE model, and especially in matters of purpose, we need to retain the perspective of people. Individual purpose is an emotional issue. Finding a sense of purpose is vital to personal happiness. It should come as no surprise then that finding a sense of purpose at work is vital to employee engagement. The relation between individual and collective purpose affords a strong tie between an organisation and its people, and when it is harmonious it yields tremendous mutual benefit. This is not an argument for making individual and collective purposes one and the same. What is essential is that they are compatible and complementary, that they create harmony and not dissent.

If purpose is for everyone, then how do you go about deciding what will excite your employees about your organisation, and how they can fulfil their own ambitions while they are part of it? This means observing your organisation in the context of society, and your people in the context of their lives.

What do we all want?

Where does a sense of personal purpose kick in? Like some organisations, it does not necessarily happen at the start of our lives. Personal purpose develops in our minds as we grow up. Throughout our childhood, if we are lucky, we are encouraged to develop talents and skills, to play to our strengths and to follow our dreams. In the countless discussions I've had and heard about education, whether for myself or for my children, the most powerful advice I have encountered is 'Find something you love', or 'Do something you're good at.' The same applies to work: identify your strengths and let them lead. I was also brought up with a strong sense of self-reliance and responsibility, meaning that I pursued my chosen activities in a way that would at least 'make a living' and at best 'make a difference.' These are the building blocks for my own sense of purpose, and I see them reflected in others and repeated over generations of family, friends and colleagues.

People often say that when they find and follow purpose, they feel empowered. It gives them a framework to act in, a goal to strive for, a moral compass to guide them through changes and decisions and moments of doubt. Once defined, it may reset people's values and behaviours and therefore affect everything they do. A sense of purpose, or fulfilment of purpose, may also lead to positive emotion and happiness.[18] Purpose is a dynamic motivation in our lives, a driver for consistency and yet also for change. It is something that people revisit at different stages of their lives according to their personal needs and circumstances.

Looking back on my adult life, I see that my sense of purpose expressed itself quite differently when I was twenty-one than it does today, in that it was much more singular and self-focused. I longed to do something important, that mattered to other people, and that I would be recognised for. For me, discovering that a job could be a vehicle for meeting such fundamental needs was fortunate, it was a blessing, and it came early. Since then, whether single, married, as a parent or as an individual, work has been for me a constant source of identity and meaning.

Fortunately, somewhere along the way I developed a sense of other people's needs and of social responsibility. From a professional perspective, I began to grasp the impact that powerful communications could have on company performance and that great individuals could have on their teams. My skill was in communication, and I took that as far as I could, but my purpose evolved into a desire to have an impact: specifically, to make people and their employers more successful. I also wanted people to recognise the link between my contribution (better communications, for example) and their own success. I wanted them to realise the value of what I had to offer. I still do.

Reading and research into the science of personal purpose often leads to Maslow's renowned Hierarchy of Needs, a model of human motivation that has been taught and applied widely across behavioural and organisational psychology. Abraham Maslow presented five levels of needs – physiological, safety, social, esteem and self-actualisation – as a progression that drives personal aspiration and motivation. He identified the desire to achieve self-actualisation (essentially to fulfil one's potential) as the ultimate goal. Created in the 1940s and refined by Maslow over twenty-five years until his death in 1970, the model has been criticised, modified and adapted by professionals and amateurs in management and employee-engagement theory.

What I liked about the model when I first came across it was that it made me think about different aspects of human motivation, and how people might be wrestling with them at different stages in their lives. What I did not like was the idea of a strict hierarchy – i.e. that you might not acquire self-esteem if you did not have material wealth, and that you could only progress to the higher levels when you had achieved the lower ones. Others criticised its lack of cultural and social sensitivity.[19] Also, when applied to organisations, I thought that it didn't quite work, as the model is so self-focused.

Maslow never presented his model in the pyramid that has become the emblem of his work, and he recognised that his original model from the 1940s was a partial, imperfect view. In later years he explored a level beyond self-actualisation that brought in a higher, more altruistic goal that people would seek to share with others. He introduced the dimension of the individual in the context of their community, and of a motivation to act in the interests of a group. Clearly this further human motivation has huge potential to drive the collective power of people, often organised in workplaces. According to Maslow, individuals who achieve personal and collective goals reach a higher sense of fulfilment and happiness, and they will be able to sustain that effort for longer. For most people, working alone delivers limited returns, and creates the incentive to find like-minded others with shared motivations and values that drives them to join organisations.[20]

Purpose at work and in life is an intensely personal matter, and to address it in the workplace requires an atmosphere of trust and mutual respect. Followers of the PRIDE model will need to strike the balance between showing interest and invading privacy, as well as to allow for different generational preferences. In my experience there are baby boomers who choose to create a sense of separation between their work and home lives, and members of later generations who are more and more vocal about what they are seeking in life and the decisions they will make to get it. I believe this is one of the dimensions of people that has most changed with the millennials, although it is not the only factor in play.

To enter into exploratory conversations is likely to pose a credal dilemma to those corporate leaders who tend to adopt a global, top-down perspective and whose instinct is to eliminate emotion. By taking a formal approach and using formal language, they risk dehumanising even this most deeply personal of topics. But a challenge faces individuals too, who may not be used to talking like this with colleagues or with bosses. Not everyone wants to share their innermost feelings in the workplace.

In summary, I urge any individual seeking satisfaction at work to identify what it is that they are able to do, what they do well, and what makes them happy, and to find other people to work with who share their passions. On the other side of the fence, I encourage every employer to take the time to get to know their employees and identify some of the core motivations that create personal purpose among them, and to then work out how their organisation can meet those needs. When people are more in tune with their own and each other's feelings, and have the confidence to articulate them, they can live and work together more easily and more productively.

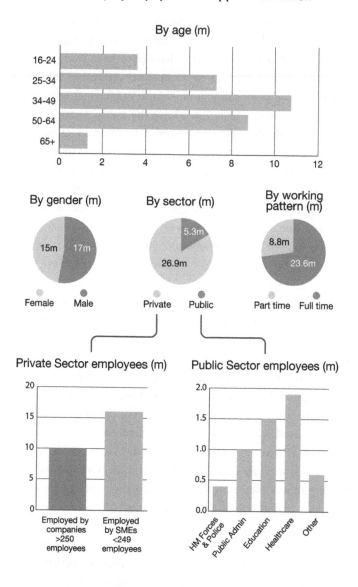

UK Employment Demographics – A snapshot
Total employed population: approx. 32 million

By age (m)

16-24	
25-34	
34-49	
50-64	
65+	

0   2   4   6   8   10   12

By gender (m)

15m 17m

Female   Male

By sector (m)

5.3m
26.9m

Private   Public

By working pattern (m)

8.8m
23.6m

Part time   Full time

Private Sector employees (m)

20
15
10
5
0

Employed by companies >250 employees   Employed by SMEs <249 employees

Public Sector employees (m)

2.0
1.5
1.0
0.5
0.0

HM Forces & Police   Public Admin   Education   Healthcare   Other

Statistics published by ONS 2018 and Department for Business, Energy & Industrial Strategy 2017

Why people create and join organisations – a personal experience

In the UK alone, about 32 million people go to work every day (see table). They are vital to the success of their employers' organisations and to the health of the economy. What drives 16 million people to join one of 5 million small or medium-sized enterprises (SMEs), a further 10 million people to join one of the 7,000 larger companies, and almost 6 million people to work for the public sector? For the individual, the answer lies in the need for fulfilment of purpose, whether financial or intellectual, and in finding the path to achieve it. For the employer, the answer lies in defining and then voicing their organisation's purpose so that it attracts the right employees, and then delivering it in everything their organisation does, in order to retain them. Achieving purpose provides meaning that may reach far beyond the material contract between employer and employee. Very often, coming to work is the way for both parties to achieve more together.

This was a key motivation in my decision to set up a company in 2001. At that time I was taking on ad hoc communications projects, but I realised I wanted to achieve more than I could on my own, to reach more organisations and impact more people. I knew that to do all I wanted meant gathering allies, building strength in numbers. Once the company existed and we won more clients, I had more responsibilities to meet and a reputation to maintain. I soon recognised that my own success relied on the commitment and performance of the whole team, and this made me even more curious about what motivates people at work. I have learned from employing others that each individual has their own sense of self and society, and that while they are contributing to a common purpose and the success of the business, they have aims and ambitions of their own to fulfil. I have always tried to know and understand my employees as individuals, to seek opportunities for them to attain their goals at work, and to celebrate their individual and collective achievements.

In considering an organisation's purpose, the starting point is, of course, what it was created to do and the benefits of its product or service. In the case of my own company, theblueballroom, which I founded in 2001, our starting point was to provide communications consultancy and materials to companies that had a large number of employees and wanted them to be informed and motivated by their company's strategies and goals. Our first goals were to win business from some prestigious clients, to devise powerful campaigns that would shine fresh light in employee communications and create excitement alike for our company and for our profession. But as we developed our offering, we, as a bunch of project managers, business writers and designers, grew ever more fascinated with the behavioural impact our work was having, not just in the narrow dimensions of communications objectives but on the broader scale of people at work.

We started to voice our purpose in terms of the impact good communications could have, first on the culture and then on the performance of our client organisations. To 'make work better', and later 'inspiring better business', became our organisation's social purpose. We expressed this widely and often inside the company, to employees and potential employees, as well as to our clients, seeking evidence and proof that our work delivers value.

Now working independently again, I continue to be motivated by the purpose we established at theblueballroom, and am proud that a desire to create words and pictures developed into something much more wide-reaching. Through raising the profile of communications inside organisations, by promoting good communications practices and behaviours and proving the commercial benefit of our work, I believe we have done a service to our clients' brands, their reputation and their people. Improving conditions in the workplace is irrefutably good for the economy and society; it is equally good for individuals.

Working for a purposeful organisation

Through my working life, I have been fortunate to know several organisations – some of them my own clients – where organisational and/or social purpose is deliberate, communicated consistently and delivered passionately: Addaction, Deutsche Post DHL, Diageo, EY, the NHS, the Armed Forces and Help for Heroes are a few of the outstanding names in this arena. They represent charities and corporates, the private and public sector, and they are strong examples of purpose in practice. In all these organisations, purpose is linked to strategy, products and services, systems, roles and people, and it is visible on the inside and the outside.

Addaction has a very clear social purpose in that it exists to help people take back control of their lives, to rebuild relationships and to become successful. And according to former HR Director and then Acting CEO Guy Pink:

in order to do that we really need our people to be compassionate, determined and professional. I feel that an organisation's purpose and values provide a kind of identikit of the type of person we want to join us. But of course nobody in reality actually looks like that identikit. They take on the organisation's purpose and values and they interpret them in a way that is authentic to them.

In my experience, particularly at Addaction, people do things really well when they care about what they are doing, when they have clarity of direction and the freedom to act. They demonstrate pride in what they are doing, without even identifying it as such. They are simply completely in tune with the organisation's purpose and values and acting with utter authenticity. Corporations and individuals tend to talk in different terms, but all people want to hear is authentic and honest communication. Individuality is such a vital thing in our relationships as much with our service users as it is with our staff. We need people to share our values at their core, to embrace them wholeheartedly, but then to be allowed to get on with being who they are.

In a completely different and more compliant business environment, financial consultancy EY regards its purpose statement as a potentially unifying watchword for its 200,000 employees across the world. Launched just over four years ago, 'Building a better working world'[21] has been systematically pursued in a massive organisational change programme, from the inside out, and right across the business, its service offering and all forms of stakeholder engagement. Alongside its established audit, tax and financial services, the firm is now consulting on transformational change, having partnered in the US with Simon Sinek, author of the best-selling business book *Start with Why*.[22] The 'Why' platform helps organisations achieve innovation, growth and operational excellence through enacting their purpose. CEO Mark Weinberger speaks eloquently about the importance of putting purpose at the very heart of EY's own business, and of engaging with employees at all levels of the organisation to explore and explain how it matters to them. The EY position is that there is mutuality in the contract between employer and employee: individuals can use the talents they have, be rewarded personally, develop new skills, and at the same time contribute to organisational goals and purpose.

Extending the concept of the individual employee aspiration is the premium drinks firm Diageo, whose purpose is 'celebrating life every day everywhere'. Their communications are clear about the company's aims to recruit people who are inspired to deliver great results, and work towards its purpose, yet they also aspire to 'create an environment where our people can be the best that they can be by ensuring everyone does work *that they see as meaningful*'. By placing the individual's sense of meaning at the heart of its own purpose statement, Diageo displays its respect for its employees and their ambitions, and makes a strong appeal to the attitudes and priorities of millennials. The message in the recruitment process touches on the exchange of skills not only for opportunity, but also for community; it demonstrates to candidates that they can fulfil some of their own ambitions and at the same time achieve a broader goal with like-minded people. The company emphasises that individuals will discover 'unparalleled opportunities' and 'a place where people are learning every day', while making their own tangible contributions to the collective purpose. Diageo presents a working contract with a sense of mutuality, celebrating organisational performance on a par with personal fulfilment.

My closest and longest association with a commercial organisation with purpose is that with Deutsche Post DHL Group, the global logistics giant, a former employer and long-time client. With operations in over 220 countries, the group is one of the most geographically and culturally diverse organisations in the world. Its employee base of more than 500,000 people is diverse too, and includes hundreds of thousands of mailmen and women in its domestic market of Germany, as well as couriers and warehouse staff, logistics and transportation experts, working around the world in gritty operational locations. As a market leader and major global B2B and B2C brand, it also employs experts in fields such as IT, digital and e-commerce, innovation, sales and marketing, finance and procurement, law, HR and communications.

Since emerging out of the financial crisis of 2008–9, Deutsche Post DHL Group has been rated by global financial markets and analysts as a successful global business. Its CEO, Frank Appel, a neurobiologist with an MSc in chemistry and former McKinsey consultant, has often impressed the markets with his strategic intellect and tenacity, but what has perhaps surprised observers of the intensely corporate world he inhabits is his strong sense of humanity and desire to make a positive impact on the world. In an interview with Frank Appel in October 2017, I asked him to reflect on the concept of purpose and how he has brought it to the centre of his leadership strategy at Deutsche Post DHL.

Appel's sense of purpose is grounded in his personal philosophy and early experience of work.

I firmly believe we have three basic needs as individuals. We are looking for someone to share our life with, someone to love; we want to serve a purpose and a greater good; and we want to have the hope that tomorrow is going to be better than today. I learned at McKinsey that this desire for purpose fed into work as well, and that my job was not about making money, it was about helping clients to become better, about making a difference. I always found that rewarding, and I discovered that other people did as well.

Setting a strategy back in 2009–10, that aimed to make Deutsche Post DHL 'the Post for Germany and the logistics company for the world', entailed ambitious strategic plans for each division and business unit and a host of implementation plans, guidelines and processes. But Appel knew that the company would also need to make huge commitment to make sure the message reached as many people as possible, and that there must be a compelling statement.

I believe people already sensed they are part of something bigger at work, but I felt it was important to be explicit about what our purpose as an organisation really was, what we achieved for our customers, and what sort of impact we have. After a great deal of thought and discussion, we came up with the concept of 'Connecting People, Improving Lives'. The strength of this statement is that it works truly and authentically for our business. It is logical and accurate, as it describes what we physically do; and yet it touches people emotionally because it also reflects the impact.

The challenge of inculcating the purpose statement across such a diverse organisation is considerable, but Appel points to the role of leadership, training and communication.

First, it is up to the senior leaders and influencers in the organisation to make work meaningful and to show employees why they can make a positive difference.

People do not always see purpose in the same way. For example, it is a fact that providing a mail service is fundamentally important for the stability of democracy in our country, or any country, in that our mailmen and women protect the confidentiality of letters. But individuals doing their job don't see it like that every day and they don't always think about it. We have to have the head, the heart and the guts to lead. 'Providing purpose' is one of the leadership attributes that comes from the heart, and as such it will appeal to the heart of our employees. A sense of purpose can really inspire people, and as leaders we have to be able to articulate that.

According to Appel, it goes against the grain for some people to speak about purpose – some middle managers, for example, because they see it as a matter for philosophers, and too emotional.

People tell me they like to hear me talking about it, but they are not so keen about talking about themselves. So we have included a whole module about purpose into our group-wide 'Certified' training programmes, so they learn how to talk about it then, in a way that is relevant to them and their teams.

The company also conducts regular and widespread communications programmes to bring awareness of the purpose statement into working lives.

You have to remind them and repeat, repeat, repeat. We communicate it all the time in training and communications channels. We are not one hundred per cent there yet. Not everyone will remember the exact words, or say them the same way, but the majority understand the sense of what it means and are proud to be part of it'

Beyond their own role at work, employees can also get involved in the company's purpose outside of the workplace through its Global Volunteer Day (GVD) programme, which benefits local communities. Employees can also contribute by getting involved in Deutsche Post

DHL's corporate citizenship partnerships with Teach for All and SOS Children's Villages.

In a year of record share prices, Appel has the fundamental belief that a purpose-led strategy, underpinned by core values, has boosted the company performance. From the beginning, he asserted a commitment to achieve triple bottom-line success – that is for shareholders, customers and employees. But not everyone was on the same page:

When we launched Strategy 2015, this was a challenge. But we have proven to our stakeholders that the triple bottom line really works. When people ask me how we have gained market share, I will tell them engaged employees lead to satisfied customers which leads to growth and happy investors.

Few companies in the world will ever reach the scale and scope of Deutsche Post DHL Group, but most leaders wishing to introduce new thinking will face similar detractors, issues and challenges. Finally, I asked Frank Appel what advice he would give other CEOs and influencers in smaller organisations on the way to introducing the concept of purpose to drive performance and engagement.

The most important thing is authenticity. You have to believe in purpose yourself and role-model it. As I said in the beginning, I believe in love, hope and purpose, I really believe it in my own life, and that's the reason I can talk about it. As soon as you understand the importance of these things, then you can talk about them and you will be convincing.

If you talk about employee engagement and never go out and do the jobs in the company, if you never do training because you think you are too smart for it, you will not engage people. If you are saying something uncomfortable, that you don't really believe, people smell that straight away. You have to live up to your own principles, and if you don't do that, you have to stop talking about them. You have to believe in what you are communicating. You just have to be authentic.

Companies like Deutsche Post DHL and other large employers in competitive markets, such as financial services, business consultancy, pharmaceuticals, engineering and FMCG, are tending to shape the topic of purpose. Here the war for future talent is felt most acutely, and purpose has become another means of differentiation and talent attraction. But the impact and benefits are much wider. It is a powerful, unifying force in organisational direction and culture, and a primary factor in driving outstanding performance.

Action Plan for Purpose: How to map out your organisation's purpose

Between an SME like theblueballroom and global giants such as Unilever and P&G, there are myriad organisations of different magnitude and with different types of impact on society. Many have already voiced their purpose, are broadcasting it to internal and external stakeholders, and are claiming commercial and social benefits as a result. So how do you join them? How do you unite all these threads to spell out the purpose of your organisation?

The process I have created is based on a simple system that aims to break through complexity and to define your work in terms of the value it delivers to society. It allows you to map out the various needs and desires of individuals and society, and enables you to plot your own and other organisations against them, according to the different type of value delivered.

Expressing purpose can elicit emotional and subjective responses, but the system is designed to rule out all implications of hierarchy or superiority. During this process, you may debate what is essential to all and what counts with individuals. The process is designed to be as inclusive and democratic as possible and accommodate any organisation that is, at the least, legal. The aim is not to judge one purpose to outweigh another, but to demonstrate how many, different organisations can anchor their activity to fundamental societal and human needs.

1. The big picture

Begin with a scene-setting exercise to create a view of societal needs that plots a context for your own organisation's activity. Write down all the needs that you perceive to exist in society as a whole. They may include physical and infrastructure essentials, such as healthcare and education, housing and utilities, safety and protection, food and drink. Then think about individual demands and desires, such as transportation, entertainment, emotional and spiritual wellbeing. Group the needs into logical areas and use these as a backdrop.

2. Who does what for whom?

Next, start to explore where particular sectors or other organisations meet particular needs. You will see clusters or spheres of activity that may appear very different yet serve similar societal/individual needs. Focus now on the particular sector that you operate in and you should begin to see where your organisation may fit, and start to identify its organisational purpose.

3. Today or tomorrow?

Now think about how society is changing and whether needs that are relevant now will be relevant in the future. Does your organisation meet the current scenario, and/or is it moving into the future? Think about which sectors work in which area, and along what timeline. This dimension of time allows you to place your organisational purpose in terms of supporting the status quo, solving essential problems or meeting current needs, as opposed to pursuing exploration, discovery and disruptive innovation that will define or serve aspects of our future society.

4. Where do you fit?

The next stage is to work through the activities your organisation is engaged in, the impact they have, how that relates to the needs of society. Are you able to voice the value that your organisation delivers to society? Are your products and services intrinsically connected to a societal need?

Because you represent the organisation that seeks to define its purpose, you may have a very clear idea of where you fit, and that is a great starting point, but it will not be the same for everyone. Be prepared to work through a process that involves people at different levels and with different experience of your organisation. Employees and consumers all have their own perspective on the world they live and work in, and according to their personal value set they will challenge or change your view of the organisation's position. Involving your employees in this mapping exercise will also prompt them to explore how they define what they value in life, and provide the context for them to spell out their individual motivations.

5. How does your purpose determine the way you operate?

As you begin to voice your organisation's intrinsic or higher purpose, think about how your organisation currently delivers its services, and discuss whether the way it operates meets its purpose. Does your organisation operate differently from others that provide the same thing, and if so, how useful is that thought for future positioning, internally and externally? Challenge your own thinking and be open to others'. In order to reach a consensus, do you need to make any adjustments to your core purpose, or to the way you run your business?

6. Spell out individual purpose

Having created some hypothetical purpose statements for your organisation, the second part of the exercise is to explore the theme of individual purpose with your present employees. People work for organisations whose purpose they respect and with people whose values they share. You will do well to explore how far your employees align with your declarations of organisational purpose and the way you wish to do business.

The scale of this process hinges on the size of your staff, but it will teach you more about the people who work for you and how their personal value-sets square with your organisational identity. If you have very few employees, for example as a start-up, you may already know a lot about the individuals who are working with you, and feel fairly confident that you know each other's minds. Nevertheless, enhancing your understanding of the personal motivation of your employees will offer greater scope for engagement and equip you for future growth.

In larger organisations, you may already have introduced personality profiling according to the job roles, culture and needs of your business, and used this to recruit and manage your employees. But if not, you should gather input from a representative number of people. Conversations with your team need to take place in a safe, non-judgemental environment, and you may decide to enlist an outside adviser to manage the discussions. In all cases, you should explain the background of this project and what you are trying to achieve.

Remember the fundamental questions covered in this chapter, around making a living, making a contribution, making an impact. Depending on their life stage or career development, employees will have a more or less demanding set of expectations about purpose. For example, if they are seeking the opportunity only to make a living, they could conceivably be drawn to any one of the activity spheres. Employees' motivations will also vary a lot according to their financial position, and whether they have other responsibilities and dependants outside of work. Yet they may well be drawn to one sphere over another because it responds to something else in their set of personal needs.

When you have identified your organisation's position, along with your employees' motivations, you can begin to grasp how the pursuit of your purpose appeals to and complements the needs and desires of the people who work for you. The ideal outcome of this process is to establish areas of compatibility in their motivation and values, so that individuals and organisations can work towards achievements and goals that appeal to them both.

7. Match your organisational principles with your purpose

The benefits of exploring purpose include greater mutual understanding between teams, an increased sense of self-awareness and self-respect, and a shared commitment to complementary goals.

Defining purpose is just one step. Living and proving your purpose in your daily business life is the harder reality. Before promoting it to customers and employees, your organisation's claims must carry conviction. You will need to examine your organisation's strategic direction, to consider how your organisational goals and targets fit the purpose, and to build the operating model to achieve them. It may be necessary to revisit or perhaps even create new products and services, processes and systems, that will enable you to deliver success to your customers, shareholders and employees, and at the same time to progress towards your purpose for people and society.

How does Purpose fit into the PRIDE model?

The PRIDE model starts with purpose because that is what underpins why an organisation exists, what it will deliver and how it will operate. It is also a universal and essential factor of human motivation.

Organisations with purpose are more attractive to customers and employees. They build recognition and reputation in the consumer and employer markets. To deliver on your purpose, you will need to voice the factors that will determine the experience of stakeholders both inside and outside your organisation, i.e. the integrity of your reputation. You will then need to find the people with the right skills, behaviours and attitudes to join your team, and motivate them with direction and energy to stay.

Employees will be motivated to join and stay with you when they believe that by fulfilling the organisation's purpose, they may also fulfil their own. The recognition of this mutual benefit lies at the heart of the dynamic relationship between employer and employee; it evokes strong emotion and is the basis on which to build pride.

2
Reputation

For good commercial reasons, reputation sits high on every corporate agenda. Derived from direct and reported experience of a company's products, services, brand and public presence, reputation drives market perceptions of a company's standing in the world. It has a direct impact on key metrics of an organisation, from share price and brand value to customer behaviour and advocacy. According to recent studies, corporate reputation accounts for 38 per cent of the market capitalisation of the UK FTSE 350.[1] Companies with great reputations are not only worth more than those without, they are also more likely to win investment from shareholders, access borrowing from banks, survive crises, gain and retain consumer trust. And there is a direct correlation between improving reputation and increasing customer recommendation.

Reputation also has a pivotal role to play in an employee's relationship with the organisation: plainly tremendous benefit ensues when an employee feels pride in a company's reputation; by the same token, a company's reputation relies, with every passing day, on the opinions, claims and behaviours of its employees. And aside from all the effort and energy devoted to building reputation in the external, customer markets, a whole industry – my chosen industry – has been born that is dedicated to the kind of engagement that spurs the positive proof of a brand promise by that brand's employees.

In the early days of theblueballroom, I felt like a disciple for the industry, championing the equality of employee communications against the dominant forces of marketing and customer communications. Employee communications, where it existed at all, was focused on information about what went on inside the company, enabling employees to do their jobs better. It was a fairly transactional process, famously tagged in some organisations as a 'need to know' or necessary evil. Now, years on, we understand much more about the emotional attachment employees feel for their brand, and the vital role of reputation in cementing that attachment. Some research goes as far as to say that brand reputation is an emotional bond that will ensure employees are engaged and deliver on strategy.[2] There is truth in this, but it is by no means the whole story, and I would like to look further back into the process of how employee–employer relationships are formed, to the times of pre-employment and pre-application, and the point when a prospective employee is simply an uninformed consumer, and the potential employer simply another name.

I believe that reputation of that name is a crucial factor, often the first point of influence in employees' and prospective employees' perception and engagement with a brand. Whether they are aged sixteen or sixty, people not only want to buy from a reputable company, they want to work for one too. Reputation creates desire, aspiration, excitement for both consumers and prospective employees. In the employment market, therefore, the prestige of your organisation's name can stir up individual ambition to join in and motivation to commit more effort and personal drive to share success – and hence it is at the heart of the PRIDE model.

In this chapter I shall examine the elements that drive reputation and present the case for fostering a strong employer brand that complements a customer proposition. I shall also consider some of the challenges that can enhance or damage company reputation, including the power of the media, and increasingly social media, and learn from successful companies who tell a consistent story across the customer and employment markets. I will argue that there is a huge opportunity to solve important recruitment and engagement challenges by bringing HR and marketing closer together to create a more cohesive brand story and then provide tips on how to deliver it.

What's in a name?

Some elements of reputation can definitely be created, and to some extent managed, by a corporation. But note the qualifications there. The external and uncontrollable influences are many and varied, and they grow more complex every day. In recent years, people have been talking a lot about the democratisation of the brand – how ownership is passing into the hands of customers and the media. I don't believe a business is a democracy, but I do think that dominant market players and the people who run them are now compelled to take more notice of the people who matter to their businesses – whether they are customers, shareholders, employees or the media.

Let's look at some of the factors that it is possible to manage. The perception of a brand's core product is still the single most important factor in driving reputation, and that is good news for business. Great sourcing, guiding principles and robust operating practices can be laid down in manuals, drilled in through training and supervision, and implemented in design studies, offices and factories all over the world. There's no magic wand, but with the right training and working conditions, excellent people following excellent processes can deliver product credibility. Service, too – often bound up in the 'products and services' category of branding and reputation audits – is hugely influential in its own right. It can raise or ruin reputation, but there is plenty that can be done in-company to see that the right procedures and protocols are defined and followed.

Brand communications in many forms, from corporate brand campaigns and external advertising to sponsorship and content marketing, are also managed reputation-builders. As consumers ourselves, we know our favourites where image meets reality, and recognise the companies that hit the mark time and again – companies who create such a buzz for the newest and latest model that the thrill of the purchase is almost guaranteed. There's always the chance that the product won't deliver, and that has always been the case, but a great deal of consumer satisfaction is derived from purchasing an aspirational product. I think 'cognitive dissonance' –

the tension you feel when a longed-for item disappoints – was one of the first terms I learned in my early days in advertising. I remember being told as well that car advertising was aimed at existing customers as much as at potential buyers, largely to reinforce or validate their brand decision. And it is still a fact that great brand advertising is hugely powerful in building customer loyalty after a purchasing decision, as well as fuelling the wish in the first place.

Direct experience is another key driver of reputation, and from the customer's point of view that stands for every transaction or contact with the brand connected to the product consumption. This includes pre-purchasing processes and materials, the actual buying decision, experience and delivery through to post-purchasing interactions and feedback. Here lies the concept of the customer life cycle and several approaches to creating and nurturing first-rate customer relationships, where the direct experience of a brand positively impacts customer perception.

Plainly the role of the employee in the customer's brand experience is vital here. Employees who are well informed, properly equipped and enjoy a positive working environment are bound to signal greater brand attributes than those who are ill-prepared, badly managed and disengaged. The more engaged the employee in the brand, product or service, the better they will care for their customers. Employee engagement is a critical factor in delivering the brand promise, and the human face your employees turn to the world is vital to the building of brand reputation. This includes peer-to-peer recommendation, which has proven to be an effective strategy both for promoting product and attracting talent.

The pressing challenge for the corporation, however, is that no matter what the positive experience of the product, services and people, and how enviable the power of advertising spend, there are several other factors with increasing sway over consumer opinion. In recent years, following crises in trust in just about every public institution, from government and Church to banks and the media, reputation audits have identified new factors such as corporate governance and citizenship that exert a growing sway over reputation scores. How a company behaves and is perceived is becoming almost as important as what a company makes and what it says about itself.

Here's the thing, though: who is the company and how do we define company behaviour? I see it as a combination of the values that propel the behaviours of all the people who lead and work for an organisation, the policies that drive the decisions of individuals, and the sense of a collective attitude that reaches beyond the transactions of the products and services to individual customers and somehow assumes an identity or personality of its own. Yet it is individual leaders and board members and managers who make the decisions that influence huge numbers of employees and thus comprise collective behaviour.

Applied to governance, company behaviour is demonstrated in a company's respect for the law, for decency, for honesty and integrity, and how that plays out into policies and decisions on finance, transparency, ownership and rights. It applies to activities of the business over which the company has direct responsibilities and control, and where sources of influence display themselves within the organisation. Activities like compliance, risk management and governance need to lose their dull image, and functional leaders in these fields need to move into the centre of employee induction and engagement activity and raise the awareness of how vital their actions are for sustainable business.

Applied to citizenship, company behaviour is seen in how it makes a positive contribution to the wider community or manages its impact there, influencing aspects of the environment or of society, where the company can enhance or do damage. It makes itself felt within a company in terms of its own employment policies, from the most basic working conditions, such as flexibility or shift patterns, to benefits such as medical or food allowances. It also has the potential to have wider effect in the community, in areas such as education or health, either through direct funding or in partnership with or dependent on other organisations in the same space.

So whatever is conveyed in a concerted way from reputation-management departments or in corporate responsibility reports needs to be authentic. Some stories that are born inside a company and distributed to the outside world can indeed be managed, but others will go uncontrolled. What really goes on at work can become stories in themselves. They can start as anecdotes in the pub, or at the school gates, and then become incidents and examples to be shared and retold throughout communities. Tangible evidence in stories from trusted friends reaches the ears not only of customers but also of the prospective employee, and it is another part of the jigsaw that makes up a corporate image.

And here lies another and undeniable factor in a company's reputation: the role of the culprit or hero of the story. Be prepared to find that when your story hits the outside world, every tale has, at best, a hero, or at worst, a villain. Just as an individual service agent or retail assistant can influence hundreds of customers' individual experiences of your product, stories of individual achievement and success have the power to boost or harm reputation. The employee as ambassador can build emotional attachment to a brand, but the contrary is also true, and stories with senior villains or incompetents do special damage.

Executives of high-profile companies carry a heavy responsibility not just for their own personal reputation but for their employer's corporate standing too. Company leaders may win fame and fortune or hearts and minds on one day, and then lose millions on share price and pension value the next, if indicted for corruption or incompetence. Company reputation may be more than the sum of its parts, but some parts carry far more weight than others, and the negative impacts of unethical leadership stretch further and last longer than temporary lapses in share price. It is also felt powerfully inside companies, seen as a breach of trust by employees. If such stories are ignored, or questions left unanswered by company leadership, they can threaten confidence in the ethics and standards of an organisation by seeming to endorse negative behaviour.

However much care a company takes over its employee behaviours and outgoing messages to the media, there is a brave new world in the public domain, where people are forming their own opinions about your corporation, based on experience, and choosing to share them. What others say about the company, in customer testimonials or peer reviews and in the media, are the other very powerful forces that influence your organisation's reputation.

The most powerful force to enter reputation management in recent years is social media. With the blurring of lines between internal and external stakeholder communications, peer recommendation and review can come from inside and outside the organisation, from analysts, journalists, bloggers, consumers and employees, and can impact the internal or external brand reputation of the business. While some of the brightest and best in brand management are creating pure entertainment in their brand stories, which social media channels lap up and amplify, others succumb to the modern malaise of 'No comment' and allow their reputation to dwindle through lack of interest or nous or both. Not engaging with your customers in the way they choose amounts to turning a deaf ear, and therefore losing the power to make suitable responses.

Customer testimonials in the media, or on websites that were once also managed, have given way to uncensored peer recommendation on numerous social peer-to-peer review sites, for example TripAdvisor and Trustpilot. It seems to me that there has always been reputational risk in inflated promises, but with communications channels too numerous and beyond the old control, the potential and pain of being found out and publicly pilloried is now definitely more acute.

The message, of course, is that while some aspects of reputation can be managed by corporations, more influence comes to light in the marketplace through the reports and activities of powerful individuals: namely customers and employees. With more people engaging with accessible channels and social media, there has been an undeniable shift in the power of the brand manager vis-à-vis the consumer. While much is written about this in the area of consumer branding, it is far less well explored in the area of employer branding.

And even when companies do involve their employees in their branding activity, it is largely tied to positioning an employee as an advocate of your brand, telling a story to the outside world to buoy up the consumer-brand performance.

With the exception of a few hundred outstanding and high-performing companies, it seems to me that when most organisations consider the employer brand they see it from quite a narrow perspective, focusing on how their employees deliver on brand reputation rather than how that attracts them to the company in the first place. Some concentrate their efforts on defining the way employees should provide the product or service, how their behaviours will reflect the preset values of the brand; others measure employee engagement with brand values and confidence in the company's brand promise to its customers. Few are considering the next step – that is to promote the brand to potential and existing employees with a view to enticing talent, and engaging employees more closely from the start.

While the more common approach recognises the solid connection between individual performance and reputation, it reduces the role of the employee to a conduit of something bigger or more important, merely reflecting brand reputation rather than being at the centre of it. This approach to employer branding with its incumbent terms such as brand ambassadors, and more recently brand advocates, begs the important question: 'What's in it for me?'

I believe the answer lies in defining a deal for employees and demonstrating it to the outside world in parallel with other brand communications. There is an enormous opportunity for companies to extend the view of the employee's relationship with the brand or organisation back to and even before the moment when people seek jobs, and to adopt a more integrated brand-reputation strategy that embraces potential employees as closely as potential consumers. This involves recognising that there is a huge overlap between brand advocacy to potential and existing customers and smarter talent acquisition and development through brand advocacy to potential employees. A more holistic approach to establishing and communicating what the company really stands for, including its offering as an employer, would buoy up strategic success, and yet very few organisations are really doing it.

Bringing people into your brand strategy

In PwC's 17th Annual CEO Survey, published in early 2014, there were the first signs of cautious optimism on the potential for global economic recovery, with half of CEOs expecting to increase headcount in 2014.[3] And yet 63 per cent of all global business leaders highlighted access to skills as a major obstacle to growth. A staggering 93 per cent of CEOs surveyed said that 'they recognise the need to make a change, or are already changing, their strategy for attracting and retaining talent. Yet 61% of CEOs haven't yet taken the first step.' These findings went along with criticism of the HR function, which was viewed as historically incapable of adopting a new strategic approach to resource planning and talent management. HR, its critics claim, needs to step up to the plate. I believe this approach is missing the point.

When challenged, most company leaders will maintain that the future success of their business relies on two major factors: the ability to drive product and service innovation to meet changing market and consumer demand, and the capability and culture of the people inside the company to deliver the brand promise. If this is the case, as it surely is, then leaders need to think strategically about how companies build, create and earn reputation with potential employees. In times of economic recovery, this is the stakeholder group that will play the critical role in delivering both innovation and service, and HR should not be alone in this task. The ability of a company to build reputation belongs to the collective leadership – the board.

While the concrete task of recruiting the right people at the right time lies with HR, there is surely a wider duty for the company leadership as a whole to make the strategic connection between brand and people, and therefore take responsibility for building a proposition that offers meaning and value to its customers *and* its employees. Attracting talent is just a part of a wider requirement in smart businesses, namely a coherent and honest people strategy. This should be a wholly joined-up policy that looks at resource planning alongside business development; that determines which people with what type of skills and capabilities the business needs to serve, deliver, grow, develop, excel; and, crucially, spells out what the business will offer in return in terms of reward, benefits, working conditions, opportunity and development.

All companies need to find the people who fulfil the customer promise today and develop the customer promise of the future. In order to find those like minds and like souls to join and stay in your organisation, you need to create conditions that will appeal to them, and then communicate their presence in a way that resonates both inside and outside the organisation.

Only when the core understanding sinks into the leadership, that the employer brand proposition needs to be multidimensional and collectively owned, will CEOs begin to conquer the 'Talent Challenge'.

Who leads the field in attracting talent?

As a start line for developing an attractive employer brand, company leaders would do well to look at the names appearing regularly in rankings of high-performing brands and high-growth businesses. It is obvious that brands with the greatest global reach and highest perceived value, simply by being known names, will attract greater numbers of applications, but a look behind the name and into their broader branding activity will reveal a huge amount of effort being spent on building attractive employee propositions as well.

These are all big employers working in highly competitive, crowded market places such as consultancy, banking, pharmaceuticals and FMCG. All need to attract high-calibre candidates to perform in current and future markets, and so they have created tangible benefits to employees that match what they offer outside. In those companies where HR and marketing are working together, and on an equal strategic footing with the CEO, great things can be achieved in brand positioning across extended stakeholder groups. A particularly cohesive scene emerges in those companies where the organisational barriers – silo mindsets – between the HR/people and marketing/customer functions have been well and truly broken.

League tables of the most attractive employers, whether European, global, or in the local UK market, will come up with a handful of dominant companies that appear across the board: big, strong, successful brands that have created a cohesive employee value proposition and put it across effectively are gaining recognition. There is a massive overlap at the highest level between those that achieve external brand reputation and those that readily attract the right employees.[4]

What strikes me about the current employer-brand arena, with its league tables of attractive graduate brands and great employer offerings, is that the employment market is becoming dominated by the superbrands. Those companies that have worked hardest on building big external brands are now showing everyone else how to showcase them to worthwhile recruits. They are not resting on their laurels but have realised that to survive and thrive they need to extend their appeal to those individuals who are strategic and proactive in the way they are seeking a career.

Of course, companies who depend on a steady flow of eager applicants to fuel their growth are acutely aware of the hazards in doing nothing, or marking time, because key demographic factors hover ahead. In the next twenty years, the global talent pool in several major industries (and particularly in the developed Western economies) will be shrinking, as people reaching retirement age outnumber incoming school- and college-leavers. Within the UK, this will cause a skills shortage of up to 7 million people, to bite hardest in the manufacturing, retail and public service sectors. Government and industry bodies are already considering ways to extend employment options to retain mature talent. The most conscientious employers are looking at a truly segmented approach to employer branding, and adapting their terms to suit changing working requirements all across their workforce.

There is a danger, however, of a massive polarisation of the employment market, with those with the cash to invest in the consumer brand coming off best in the war for talent. Outside of the top graduate recruiters and superbrands stand thousands of companies seeking the same great people and losing out. Most of the population are working for the thousands of companies who orbit outside this elite talent bubble, perhaps in a sector that is relatively specialist, or just unknown to the job-seeking markets. These employers have terrific strengths, and most likely a great reputation with their customers. They have a lot to offer to employees, but they have low brand awareness, and therefore minor status in the recruitment market.

Sadly, many companies – and even some of the largest and most established – still see recruitment activity as costly and frustrating, at best an adjunct to other forms of marketing, but more likely a completely separate exercise. One department manages the brand and runs advertising campaigns to customers; another turns to recruitment websites for potential employees – and ne'er the twain shall meet. With that disconnect comes confusion or lack of clarity for people who need to know what a company does and stands for. Very few companies consider their employer brand in the same light as their consumer brand, as a powerful, multi-faceted identity that offers concrete benefits and great aspirational potential in the war for talent.

A WORD TO SMES WHO ARE ASKING: 'DO I REALLY NEED TO DO THIS?'

SME companies represent 90 per cent of all companies in the UK and they create 50 per cent of new job opportunities, yet employer-brand activity remains dominated by the superbrands. If you are or aspire to be one of those high-growth companies and have no employer-brand strategy, then you are going to miss out on the best and the brightest recruits. Reputation in any market – whether with customers, investors or employees – has to be worked at. Don't be content with the applicants you are dealt – get out there and fight for the best. You and your business need to find them, and if you are really driving the UK economy forward, you deserve to hire them.

Breaking into the employer-brand elite

Building a consumer brand from scratch should entail everything you stand for, from your products, services, market positioning and customer experience through to culture and values, individual and collective behaviours that are undergone by customers and recognised in the media. All of this helps to create a reputation that will keep existing customers happy and attract new ones. The brightest and the best brands are thinking this way when they come to recruiting too.

People or departments currently speaking on behalf of companies, whether corporate communicators, brand marketers or media spokespeople, have a huge opportunity to make an impact. They should take all that they know and care about in relation to external stakeholders' motivations and roll the interests of employees and potential employees into every aspect of brand-reputation management. That way, existing employees will feel properly respected from outside, and when people first approach the company as potential employees, they will have a sharper sense of what the company stands for, not only as a supplier, but also as a prospective employer.

Companies without an articulated employer brand now have the chance to define that proposition, check how it suits the existing brand identity, gather evidence dictated by the reality of working in the organisation, and put it across in a way that responds to the employment arena. In order to strengthen your company's employer brand, let's track the journey of a potential employee, from the very start.

Most potential employees will have a view of the organisation's reputation that starts – like a customer's – from their own experience of the company, its advertising and external branding, and the standing it enjoys among peers and influencers. Depending on their level of experience in work, they will be more or less tuned in to the appeal of the company as an employer, will have their own expectations and needs, and be looking to learn more. Their predisposition, however, emerges from the company's reputation.

Employers looking for high numbers of newly qualified graduates, such as consultants in professional services, have started their employer-branding activity way in advance. Talent attraction starts with in-school or in-college sponsorships of curriculum and extra-curriculum activities, relating to sports, arts or culture. Internships and work-placement schemes are on offer sooner and sooner in the undergraduate career, as big companies look to build brand relationships not only with potential customers but also with the next generation of staff. And because of the long-term relationship they promise with their recruits, places are already highly competitive.

Of all sectors of the working population, graduate entry-level recruits generally enjoy the most highly developed form of employer branding, and certainly the most attention of all employee segments.

For economic reasons voiced earlier, this is not likely to change in the next two decades. The battle for new and trainable talent is waged in the thousands of dedicated websites, not only from the highly ranked professional services sector, but also from just about every listed, FTSE, Fortune, DAX, blue-chip company in the world. With limited experience of the working world, graduate entry-level employees are more likely to seek out and find information that is targeted straight at them, and so will be most susceptible to the proactive messaging that companies put out. Rarely in later life, and only then in specialist or high-demand sectors, will they ever be so actively pursued in recruitment fairs, advertising and social media campaigns that say so emphatically: 'We want you.'

First-time employees may have an idea in theory of what they want in their working life, but they don't have much practical knowledge of what that looks and feels like. They will compare terms and conditions, career and personal development opportunities, maybe even culture and values, but they won't have a backdrop of experience against which to judge the offers. They also know they are running in a fierce competition, as the number of graduates applying to known companies far outweighs the number of elite jobs available. And so they too are claiming that they will suit the scheme on offer, tweaking their CVs, coaching for online assessment tests, often without any realistic understanding of what the end job may entail. With the exception of the most sophisticated assessment-centre processes, there is a kind of matchmaking lottery that goes on, with everyone putting their best face forward, but neither side truly able to judge what is on offer, or what the future will hold if the contract is made. Offering and accepting that first job offer are acts of considerable mutual faith.

The highest-performing brands, however, communicate well with those with more experience, too. Recruitment pages for companies such as Siemens, McDonald's and Volkswagen contain detailed descriptions of what employees can expect from a career there, along with stories of successful individuals in specific roles. If a potential employee approaches a company after, for example, ten years' experience in the workplace, they clearly have more points of reference by which to gauge an employer benefits offer. Like any entry-level candidate, they will gather their data from a company's website, their recruiters, the media and their friends, but they will also have personal knowledge of prior working conditions, policies, values and behaviours that they aim either to find or avoid in a future role. If they start positively disposed towards a company, based on its reputation as a brand, they will then look beyond the prospects of the specific job, to the tangible evidence of additional benefits that company provides as an employer.

And yet recruitment activity is only part of the employer-brand story.

The most sophisticated brand leaders pay constant heed to building their reputation as good employers beyond the confines of HR policies and processes. They maximise their reputation through promoting commercial achievements and operational best practice, inside and outside the company. They follow best practice in terms of governance, operational safety, risk management and people management; and they discuss it in the public domain. They monitor their key performance indicators, carry out customer and employee surveys, follow good citizenship policies, apply for accreditations and then publish results and awards. They readily promote their position as industry spokespeople or thought leaders in vertical and business media. They wrap everything they do in the terminology of good business and employment principles, demonstrating the culture and behaviours of the organisation through their core activities and their people.

In the best-performing companies, assessed by both external and internal metrics, a coherent brand story starts on the inside and radiates far and wide. It is also an ongoing process, reaching people before they think of joining the company and continuing after they have left. Like the customer cycle, the employee cycle is a continuous loop. These companies also realise that the loops of stakeholder communications constantly overlap, and so the very best of them match the qualities and characteristics of their employer brand with their consumer brand, not necessarily in the same, but always in compatible, complementary, terms.

While creating the employer value proposition belongs to the entire leadership team, the communications responsibility for the brand story usually lands with marketing and HR. The final section of this chapter presents an approach that gathers some tips from the best examples in the field and provides a 'how to' guide to taking your offering to the employment market.

Action Plan for Reputation: Where to start with an employer brand?

Building an employer brand means developing a structured proposition for employees, that has specific requirements to enable delivery of the external brand proposition to customers and in return offers terms and conditions, benefits, opportunities and rewards that appeal to the organisation's entire employee population. The proposition should resonate with everyone who comes into contact with the company, and be communicated consistently externally and internally, in order to reach, attract and retain the best people. That employer brand will be anchored in reality but will also create the emotional appeal of opportunity and excitement for existing and potential employees.

1. What is your story?
The employer-brand story will include the company's purpose, its products and services, the relationships it has with all its key stakeholders, its direction, the opportunities it offers employees, the culture and values of the organisation and its impacts on the world. Clearly this is a substantial story, so you will need to take time to gather facts, opinion and aspiration from a lot of different people.

My experience of organisations shows that, whatever the issue, when you start asking questions it makes good sense to know why you are doing it. So if you have accepted a job that involves articulating an employer brand, start by agreeing with your boss or board a short and succinct statement, or an elevator speech that says, very simply, what it is you are doing and what you are hoping to achieve.

Defining your employer brand may, for example, differentiate your organisation in a competitive marketplace, help your recruitment issues, improve employee engagement in your strategy, drive better customer awareness or service, and deliver many other benefits. Be confident that your company has a good reason to be considering this topic. Know what the strategy is behind your project and be ready to explain it, in simple terms, wherever you go.

Once you have defined an elevator speech it's time to start your research. Go out to your key stakeholders and gather data.

2. Who needs to be involved?

Draw up a list of the factors and functions in your organisation that affect the employee's experience of the brand. It is likely that every department in your organisation will have some sort of impact on perception of employer brand, so draft a plan about how you connect with them and whom you need to talk to. In most companies, employee issues are managed by HR and branding issues by marketing, so you may need to create a project team or even steering group that can harmonise different interests and responsibilities.

Be prepared to make connections between departments that haven't traditionally cooperated, and sometimes to break down silos. Organisations are traditionally hierarchical and modular, where accountability for one thing rests with one department. People and branding cross boundaries, so it will help if you are a good diplomat and communicator. You should show understanding and respect for different perspectives, and define common ground so that your stakeholders support your project.

An employer brand also needs to represent all levels of an organisation, so you need to get access to people beyond board members or department heads. Follow the processes that are relevant for your organisation's culture, but don't get stuck in the higher echelons of the hierarchy, and keep an open mind.

3. What do you already know from the inside?

You can delve into existing data, create surveys or simply have conversations with people, but find out in a structured way what the current perceptions are in the organisation.

Questions to ask include: Does the leadership team already express an employee offering? Why do employees join, stay or leave? What did they know about the company before they joined? How has that matched their experience to date? What is their day-to-day contribution to the company brand? Do they understand, engage with and reflect the external brand proposition? What do they see as the benefits of working here? Does that match the leadership team's views? What are their aspirations?

Record your findings in a logical way and keep notes of your sources. Your understanding of the topic will develop as you progress, and sometimes it is useful to go back to people you talked to at the start of a project for further insight or follow-up conversations, with more depth.

4. What does it look like from the outside?

At the same time as investigating the inside story, you need to consider how your brand is perceived in the external employment market. You can conduct research with recruiters, headhunters, recent job candidates, sector-specific media and even customers, and then compare their impressions with the internal stakeholders.

You should also look at all the external communications channels that potential and existing employees will access. These include your website, recruitment brochures, campaigns, sponsorship activities and any other promotional activity in the community. Do you know how your employees are talking about you online or out in the world? Do you have official and unofficial pages on Facebook? How does your brand do on Glassdoor? Have you been featured in any media reports or surveys recently? What would a potential candidate find out about you online?

5. Trace the employee journey – real and aspirational

Draw up a visual or diagram of the key components of your employees' journey from pre-recruitment onwards and fill in what happens at each stage.

What is the true employment contract? How does the employee contribute to the organisation's purpose and business, and what are the benefits in return? Think about what this tells you about the company or brand, and whether this is really consistent with the external brand perceptions. What are the physical and tangible terms and conditions of work? What is the culture and mood of the company? Are its values demonstrated in other employees, peers, supervisors and leadership? Do employees feel a sense of shared purpose with the organisational goals? Are they proud to work for your organisation? This is the core of your employee value proposition.

For some organisations, there will be a lot of work to be done before the employee value proposition is ready and the employer-branding story can be written. The offer will be found wanting, or will simply not yet exist as a strategic perspective. This topic will be covered in more detail in Chapter 3, Integrity. For the purposes of this employer-branding exercise, we will now assume that your organisation has a robust employee value proposition to put forward to the outside world. And your leadership team and steering group, if you have one, have decided that the organisation is ready to articulate and promote it.

6. Put the brand into your employee-brand proposition

The creation of your employer-branding proposition should be a strategic, creative and collaborative process, combining the most important characteristics of your organisation's external brand with the expressed contribution and benefits for your employees. It should reflect strongly held beliefs in the brand and should differentiate the organisation from competitors. It needs to be authentic and meaningful to existing and potential employees and apply to all aspects of the employee experience.

There really is no set formula to creating the employee proposition, but great examples can be found in some of the world's highest-profile employers: the BBC, BP, Coca-Cola, EY, John Lewis, Mars, McDonald's, Siemens, Unilever, the Virgin Group; and the most attractive entrepreneurial and high-growth brands: Airbnb, Dropbox, Facebook, Innocent Drinks and Zappos. All of these companies have a proposition that builds on the purpose and values of the organisation, the aspirational and real benefits of working there. The core statement vocabulary and tone reflect the external brand propositions.

When you arrive at this point in the employer-brand story, carry out research into comparable and competitive organisations in your marketplace, as well as highly regarded brands in the employment arena that reflect your own or aspirational brand personality. Making your brand proposition stand out is key.

7. Communicate your employer brand

There are a number of considerations to make in communicating an employer brand, and these include stakeholder and audience segmentation, creative messaging and storytelling, and comprehensive channel selection.

Audience segmentation

This will include employees within the organisation (to share or explain existing or new offerings) as well as different target groups externally. Consider all the stakeholders who were part of your initial research, from recruiters and headhunters, influencers and media to potential candidates themselves. The messaging for all target groups needs to be consistent, but not necessarily the same. Just as your employee-brand proposition offers different benefits to different employees, so will your campaign messages be targeted and delivered to different groups.

Messaging and storytelling

In his ground-breaking book on the impact of the Internet on marketing and business interaction, *The Cluetrain Manifesto*,[5] David Weinberger and his collaborators explored the idea of the market as a place of conversation and shared knowledge, and encouraged businesses to embrace natural, human conversation as the true language of commerce. They also argued that corporations work best when the people on the inside have the fullest contact possible with the people on the outside. While focused on the conversations businesses were having with customers, the same principles can be applied to potential employees.

The digital generation has witnessed a massive trend in employer-brand communications using employees as their brand advocates and giving them the platform to tell the brand story. Accelerated by the proliferation of digital and social media, most recruitment communications activity has broadened from a top-down corporate-style party broadcast to a rich narrative of individual human experiences that can be shared more readily.

Even if candidates are unaware of the term 'employee value proposition', they will certainly be looking for its component parts, including physical working conditions, pay and performance structures, opportunities to contribute, learn, develop and advance, as well as culture and values, and additional benefits to joining that are specific to your organisation.

Choose your channels

The range of channels available to reach your audiences has increased in number and complexity, but a few core categories are worth considering. The largest source of managed content you possess should be made available on a dedicated area of your own company website, with a clear link from your home page. That in itself is the first and most likely place an incoming candidate will look for clues of your employee offering.

But driving potential candidates to your website (who may not yet have thought about your company) and proactively communicating your employer brand requires a managed media and social media campaign. Priority hits should include all the major generic and sector-specific jobsites and job boards, leading network platforms such as LinkedIn, and equivalents in other markets, for example Xing in Germany. With digital channels like YouTube being both popular and accessible, volume and variety of stories has enriched the employer-brand story and companies who embrace the opportunity of informal and user-generated video join an already rich conversation online.

A whole range of materials should be at the ready once a lead is created, and that should include candidate-recruitment packs, a defined employer-brand story narrative, an account of the component parts of your employee journey, together with explanations on process. Any materials that rely on face-to-face delivery should be accompanied by user notes and training offers for recruiters and managers.

8. Measure the impact of employer branding

There are several established benchmark surveys that have found correlation between high-achieving business performance and a strong, recognised and reputable employer brand.[6] When seeking to measure the positive impacts and return on investment (ROI) of using the PRIDE approach, companies can, as far as possible, ring-fence the activity that is involved and measure those results against the goals it has set out to achieve. So if your objective is to raise your profile within a particular market sector, then measure awareness and recall of your brand before and after you start your activity. If it is to reduce the time and cost of recruiting in a particular market, make sure you start with accurate data and identify factors that influence the outcomes. Be aware of interdependencies and build those into your measurement methods. Communications in itself is never the only influencing factor, and so a degree of common sense is required when setting your targets. An employer brand is delivered through a great employee value proposition, i.e. the integrity of the offer, as well as how it is positioned. We will continue that discussion in the next chapter.

How does Reputation fit into the PRIDE model?

If purpose brings meaning, reputation brings notoriety. Both build pride in your organisation. Potential employees will decide whether to engage with your organisation based on the strength of your reputation. Employees of reputable brands enjoy the association of fame, gain respect from their peers and take pride in the part they play.

But reputation alone is not enough. It needs to be backed up by an authentic customer and employee experience. Once involved with your organisation, employees take on some of the responsibility for maintaining that reputation through delivering to your customers. They must believe in the integrity of your reputation, before they can live up to it. If there is no organisational or brand integrity behind your reputation, there will be no foundation for employee pride.

The interdependent relationship between organisation and individual expresses itself most strongly in the areas of reputation and integrity. Employees become the human face of your brand/ organisation, and are expected as part of their contract to deliver on its customer promise; yet their ability and inclination to do so will depend on their inside knowledge and experience of working for your brand/organisation. The PRIDE model creates the essential congruity between external reputation and internal reality and that will drive performance.

WHEN REPUTATION RAISES EXPECTATIONS

Almost forty years ago, when I was a student, I had a string of regular temping jobs, and in one particularly busy summer vacation I worked at the (then) new London headquarters for a massive global brand, as a receptionist/telephonist.

Walking in to the offices at the age of nineteen, I got a huge kick out of being in such a prestigious office and working for such a prestigious brand. I still remember the layout of the reception, where I sat, to whom I reported. I remember thinking about the cinema advertisements of the time, and I expected life at work to be equally sunny and happy.

But guess what? At that particular moment life was not that positive at all. There were changes afoot, challenges to face. A lot of people weren't happy and a lot of people shared that on a daily basis with the hapless receptionist.

Of course, I had no idea why, and had little to compare it with. I certainly had no real experience of the demands of permanent work at that stage, or the major things that happened in a company to make or break the mood. But I decided then and there that, wherever I worked in the future, I needed to work with other people who were proud of their organisations and proud of what they did.

Recalling the bad memory, I am grateful for the life lesson and for the inspiration to do something about it.

What I observed there that stayed with me for years, is that however amazing it was to get a job at a renowed brand, in order to be proud of working there, there had to be some substance behind the reputation. It was one of those formative experiences that shaped the principles I made for my own working life, and I have sought real integrity ever since. It also sparked this passion I have for understanding why people work and how what I do in life can somehow 'make work better' for everyone.

3
Integrity

Once an employee accepts a job and becomes embedded in the organisation, nothing that they experience should jar or conflict with external brand reputation. Creating an employer brand that is built on a robust employee value proposition is one of the central features of the PRIDE model, as it gives employees the confidence and motivation to deliver on the brand promise to customers.

In this chapter we look at the integrity of your brand internally, and how to create a working experience in your company that elicits the best from your employees. We will consider what a good employee experience really looks like, how it can flourish from inside, so that what an organisation says and what it does are one and the same for all its stakeholders. The aim is to enable you to deliver an employee experience that continually motivates, involves, recognises and rewards people, and so gains employee commitment to achieving organisational success.

This is the area of business management and workplace dynamics that is most closely related to the consultancy I have provided to clients, both as managing director of theblueballroom until 2015, and now as an independent consultant. My approach has been derived from over twenty years' experience of working closely with some of the world's largest and most diverse organisations. It is also proven in the outstanding levels of pride and engagement that theblueballroom employees have shown in their work and their roles, through upturns and downturns, throughout those years.

Companies with brand integrity ensure that the inner truth of their organisation is as good as its outer promise. When a reputable brand has that integrity, levels of employee engagement and performance soar.

Here we take some typical episodes in a company's lifecycle and explore some high-impact moments, when the simple actions of individuals have the potential to make the difference between engagement and disengagement. We illustrate what good – and bad – looks like, and offer guidance for leaders and managers on how to set the example of habits and behaviours that deliver beneficial results.

Building firm foundations – meeting your corporate responsibilities

Setting up and running places of work carries considerable responsibility. Whether a Unilever or an Uber, a third-sector player or an SME, there is a common set of financial and legal responsibilities that organisations need to meet if they are providing services to or employing members of the public. The scale of responsibility will vary enormously according to the size of the organisation, the type of products and services it provides, and its commercial or geographical reach, but the scope is common to them all (see opposite page).

Topics like risk management, health and safety and compliance rarely ignite a leader's or an entrepreneur's passion. They are complex, they require specialist knowledge and incur costs. Yet they are vital for two reasons.

First, they contribute to the security, reputation and long-term sustainability of the organisation. They are in place to uphold the principles of legal, decent and sustainable operational practices and working environments that are fair and safe for employees. The Institute of Directors (IOD) goes as far as to say that 'good governance is an essential prerequisite for sustainable corporate success.'[1]

Second, they have a demonstrable impact on the culture and behaviour of the people in the organisation and what is accepted

---

WHAT MAKES FOR GOOD GOVERNANCE? A CHECKLIST OF CORPORATE RESPONSIBILITIES

Good governance must be in place to ensure that the organisation is operating legally, that it complies with global and local regulations, adheres to professional standards and is treating its employees fairly. Leaders should seek specialist advice on the following topics:

- Financial and legal reporting
- Public, professional and personal liability insurances
- Risk management
- Employment contracts
- Operational work environment
- Health and safety
- Security
- Code of conduct
- Compliance

Good governance is rarely considered to be core to the business. Yet it is an essential foundation of a sustainable business, will foster good practice and safeguard reputation.

---

as the norm. Organisations that respect the law, pay their taxes and promote good practices in operational health and safety are, *ipso facto*, already creating a culture of respect for all their stakeholders. Experience shows that high standards of corporate citizenship deliver further mutual benefits. While the organisation provides protection and care to employees, it also sets the bar for high individual standards that employees will follow, and this can only benefit performance.

There can also be terrible consequences when these factors are missing. Remember Alton Towers: there a failure to meet health and safety standards in June 2015 led to a rollercoaster crash that caused life-changing injuries to five members of the public, and injuries to eleven others. The scale of the damage to these individuals is incalculable. From a reputational point of view, the way the CEO responded to the accident was considered to be efficient and compassionate, yet the impacts on the company's business were severe. The owners of Alton Towers, Merlin Attractions Operations Ltd, admitted responsibility and paid a fine of £5m in 2016. In the year following the accident, there was a 50 per cent fall in profits and more than 150 job losses at the company.

For these reasons alone, I submit that whether for a founder, owner, principal, partner or member of the board, it is a vital leadership task to see that these responsibilities are met.

Every step counts: take a walk in your employees' shoes

The essence of an employee value proposition is the tangible content of their role in your organisation and the benefits they get for working for you. Starting with the job spec, and expanding into every aspect of their workplace experience, employers should convey a clear view of what their staff will be required to do, where they will be based, the physical environment they work in, who they will work with, and the pay and rewards package. You need to define all these factors to ensure they are accurately presented to your candidates, and your offer should be relevant and competitive to potential and current employees in the employment market.

Pay and reward schemes are made up of basic remuneration (salary, bonus, financial incentives), fixed benefits (such as pensions and health insurance) and variable non-financial benefits (such as extra-curricular training, discretionary time off, wellbeing offerings or community involvement). Most high-performing companies and leading brands benchmark their scheme against market and sector offerings and consider different options for different parts of their organisation; employees have the option to choose the non-financial variable benefit that most appeals to them, according to their career or life stage.

Benefit, however, is not all about pay and rewards. It also means the intellectual and emotional advantages that your company, rather than someone else's, can offer. Are you a company at the forefront of your sector? Do you offer a stimulating, innovative environment? Do you work in a more mature market, where competitive edge may come from smarter production, pricing or marketing? Do you offer employees the challenge to improve on something that is established, or the chance to create new products? Are you a start-up, asking experienced employees to take a risk by joining, yet offering potentially high rewards? Or is the company more stable, and do you need to entice fresh blood with offers of a more predictable and secure path? What is the value of your brand in the external market? Will individuals get kudos from working for you? Every company will have different benefits to offer, but take the time to define them, assess them in the marketplace and refine them if they are falling short.

The employee journey

The proposition you define needs to play out in everything an employee encounters at work during their employment with you. Some people call this the total employee experience or employee journey. I first came across the concept of that journey in a presentation by Virgin Mobile back in 1995, and I was impressed by the comprehensive way that the company defined the employment contract in terms of its brand proposition. It was only years later, when I came across the work of Simon Barrow, that I realised he was in fact the inventor of the Employment Wheel that Virgin had so skilfully adapted.[2] And he continues to do fine work in this field.

Many clients of theblueballroom created their own similar employee-experience models that combine aspects of their external brand propositions applied to internal processes and behaviours. And I have worked and learned alongside some of the biggest and best employers in the world as they have defined and implemented employer branding on a global scale. But there is still a huge gulf between best and everyday practice in business, and frighteningly few companies outside the top-performing brands have given the subject the strategic regard it deserves.

From personal experience, my preferred approach is to first look at the employee journey through a set of predetermined processes – processes that can be created by policy, measured in execution and benchmarked with others. These are the practical, rational aspects that drive employee engagement with your company and make people want to work there and be committed to their role.

Alongside the processes, we consider the more behavioural and cultural dimensions that determine an employee's experience in the workplace. These can be hard to define and even harder to implement as policy. Their success relies wholly on people's better instincts to apply policy with good grace, to show by example how to treat people with fairness and respect, and as far as they can to behave really well all the time.

Making first impressions

Begin by thinking about every contact point employees have with your organisation, from the recruitment process on: where the job was advertised, the way the application system worked, how they were briefed before and after the interview, how they received their job offer, how it was negotiated, and how you responded to their acceptance. First impressions count, so it is never too early in your relationship with potential employees to create policies and practices that stay in the mind.

Consider in advance what new recruits need in their first days and weeks in their jobs. You should have a thorough induction programme that covers what their role entails, and a timetable for how they will be familiarised with their responsibilities. How will they be managed, and if necessary trained and then developed? Key factors in early engagement are clarity of job description, being equipped with the means to perform the job, and feedback on personal performance. Don't forget that most people approach new jobs with a mix of optimism and apprehension, wanting to be successful and afraid of failure. Make sure that everyone in the new employee's team is aware that they are joining, knows what their job will be, and is given some background about them. Involving existing staff members in an induction is a great way to share the responsibility and sense of ownership, and it gives more people a voice in the way the company speaks to a new recruit.

Think about an employee's first physical impressions of the company, from their desk or workstation. Look at your premises from their point of view. Are they secure, clean and attractive to employees? Do they display the image that you want your employees to receive of your company? Are they compatible with the brand values you set out to your customers? If you are an SME or in small premises, you may think that a tour of the building is unnecessary, but everyone needs to know where they are sitting, who they are sitting next to, where the toilets are and where to get tea, coffee and lunch. Everyone wants to feel welcomed, so encourage everyone to be positive about the new recruit. If they need a specific workstation or equipment to perform their role, make sure it is available. For example, check that an email account is already up and running, show them where the printers are, how to unjam them, and tell them who knows how to change a cartridge.

The simplest orientation needs to be given to all new recruits, and pay special attention to those joining the workplace for the first time, or after a career break. It is shocking how often people will report their experiences of first days or first weeks at work in terms of being ignored by their colleagues, disconnected from their team and unaware of what is happening in their office, let alone in the company. Careless and thoughtless practices like these dampen the enthusiasm of new recruits and quickly create feelings of isolation and disengagement. Don't let the costs and energy of your recruitment efforts go to such an appalling waste.

Performance management and career progression

A job description will outline key tasks, but it doesn't set specific goals or define what individual success looks like. As they settle into their jobs, it is important for employees to understand not only what they have been employed to do but also how the company will rate their performance. Companies need to set individual targets and provide the means for people to achieve them. They should give regular feedback on individual performance, and structure rewards schemes that are based on achievable goals.

Performance appraisals should happen for all employees at least once a year, although high-performing companies make sure that feedback isn't just an isolated event in an annual appraisal session, and is built in to the regular working relationship between manager and teams. One-to-one meetings should take place all year round to discuss progress towards goals, achievements, obstacles to action and strategies to succeed. Companies need to set and adhere to their own rhythm of performance management, but it is recommended that performance meetings should be held no less than once per quarter (and preferably monthly) and that targets should be recorded, minuted and adjusted at each session.

Performance management also means helping those who are not achieving, and providing development plans, training or coaching to fill the gaps. It matters just as much to have a fair and transparent process for complaints handling, exception management and disciplinary action as it does to manage rewards. Expecting perfection leads to certain disappointment, and so mistakes need to be reviewed, understood and learnt from. Performance management also includes resource planning, matching opportunities to high achievers and enabling them to progress.

The whole area of learning and development has become a huge part of people strategy and is a key factor in achieving better talent retention and higher employee engagement. Employees will be looking for different opportunities at different stages in their lives, and motivational triggers certainly vary between generations and life stages,[3] but the opportunity to use one's skills, to learn new competencies and to make a contribution through one's work are universal factors of staff engagement. Companies should, at the very least, make sure that the opportunity for learning both in job roles and through formal training is readily available.

Establishing an appropriate communications culture

Beyond induction into their role and responsibilities, employees should be informed early on about, or be given easy access to, more general company information. This includes organisational structures, who's who, operational guidelines, customer profiles, products and services, goals and current financial performance. Of course, there are different levels of relevance and interest, and not everyone in your workforce needs the same amount of detail. However, a basic understanding of the context employees work in aids their feeling of familiarity and belonging.

Sharing the scale of the organisation, its core purpose and values, what it wants to achieve, and how it wishes to be seen in the marketplace, will add to a new employee's sense of familiarity, belonging and motivation. I knew one finance manager at a massive global firm who made sure everyone in his department was shown photos of the directors of the main financial boards, so that if they dropped in on the department, his team would recognise their ultimate bosses. He wasn't asking them to behave any better with them than with any other visitor, but the information helped them to connect with the leadership, and gave them more confidence as a result.

Whatever the level of sophistication of the company, the leadership is responsible for the overall business strategy, budget or annual plan that drives company activity. The most successful companies share these plans with their employees, and make it clear, at all levels, how individual or departmental targets fit into the bigger picture. When people are at ease in their own roles and understand how to deliver a good performance, many will look for this sort of information to work out for themselves how their role impacts other parts of the business, with whom they need to interact, and how they fit into the organisation's plan.

Don't leave this to chance. Ambitious companies need ambitious people whose drive and energy will contribute to a team or company performance. Different organisations create different operational models, but few employees work completely solo. At a certain stage, people can be incentivised to take collective responsibility for group effort. In many high-performing companies, rewards and incentives are structured in this way from the start to reflect collective as well as individual performance.

In any organisation, professional communicators can make a tangible contribution to the corporate reputation and health of their organisation by driving awareness and understanding of all aspects of organisational integrity, from governance and employment law to health and safety and compliance. They can underpin strategy by clear communications on a company's direction and future. But nowhere should the function be seen as merely carrying or formulating messages.

It is implicit in the spirit of the PRIDE model that, in those organisations where it thrives, the specialist function of internal communications will play a pivotal role in defining and delivering the essence of a company's reputation. In many ways they are the creators and guardians of the corporate story and key contributors to the organisation's culture, not solely responsible for its inner truth, but an integral part of it.

An effective internal communications function, whether reporting to the CEO, or part of the branding, marketing or HR function, should exist to support the core purpose of the organisation. A key responsibility should be to establish processes and behaviours that demonstrate a relevant and effective communications culture that will drive employee engagement and pride in the organisation. From regular face-to-face meetings and briefings through traditional and digital platforms and events, any company channels should reflect your organisation's goals and values, and meet your employees' preferences.

More and more, the HR and communications functions in leading organisations have become brokers of best communications practice and behaviour, helping people grow more connected not only to their business or organisational goals but also to each other. Desired communication skills should be defined, encouraged and developed as part of your cultural behaviour, and set and written into your leadership and management competency profiles.

All employees should also be given the opportunity to contribute to the organisation's narrative and story. Whether a highly process-driven operational company or a personally networked innovation centre, the communications processes and habits that are created by the internal communications function should enhance both the performance of the organisation and its employees' day-to-day experience. Working in a positive way between strategists and planners, managers and teams, they can indeed provide the intellectual and emotional link between the organisation's and the people's perspectives that lies at the very heart of the PRIDE model.

Leavers and alumni

Employees leaving a company, for whatever reason, should also be treated with professionalism and respect. Employers should take an interest in the reasons why people leave and where they are going. This has both direct and indirect business benefit. On the one hand, a professional exit process can provide the business with useful anecdotal information on people's impressions about it from the inside and their motivation to leave. If the company has a fairly open culture, exit interviews don't hold many surprises, but in more formal or closed environments departing employees can share opinions they have till now withheld. It's important to spot patterns as well. A department that is losing a lot of people, for example, may be on a run of bad luck or have a bad manager, and it is healthy to seek the root cause of the attrition.

But ending a contract does not have to end a relationship. Exiting employees can still be customers or shareholders, they may want to return in years to come, or they may be potential clients. Having a positive ongoing relationship with former employees, whether as alumni or informal networks, adds to your credibility as a brand. Some companies, such as Virgin, have a proactive reconnecting policy with leavers and have even implemented 'forget-me-not' schemes to invite former successful employees to return to the company if they feel they have made a mistake in taking the new job.

The employee journey, from year to year or role to role, is punctuated by multiple milestones, and usually recorded in formal HR management systems. They form the backbone of your company's people strategy and an individual's CV, but they are not the whole story. What we will turn to now is the day-to-day delivery of your brand integrity, what employees undergo in their daily work, through contact with your products, with their colleagues and with their managers. This is the experience that sorts the good days from the bad at the office, and it forms the basis of what they say informally about their work to their friends and family.

Your customers acquire their own impressions of what it is like to do business with you, and most companies put a great deal of effort into seeing that this matches their brand. Companies are generally less good at realising that brand integrity is just as important to prove to employees, and makes itself felt in everyday exchanges in the workplace. Let's shift the focus away from all the systems and checks and balances of the organisation's integrity, and think about people and behaviours. Specifically, the day-to-day experiences that employees will have when they work in your organisation, and the working style and culture they will encounter.

Work is an emotional issue

One of my earliest influences in this area of work was the communications consultant Roger D'Aprix, who worked in large US corporates in the 1980s and 1990s. He believed that the major economic crises of that era had dramatically and permanently changed the contract between employer and employee. In his book *Communicating for Change*,[4] D'Aprix sets out a series of emotions that employees go through as they get to know a company, like what they see, and eventually feel committed to play their part. To me, this represents the potential evolution for an individual from a state of employment to engagement and signals the all-important progress from the personal acceptance of a single job to a sense of collective accountability for a greater goal.

What was unusual about this book was that, at a time when the business world was obsessing about harmonisation of standards and relentless drives for process efficiency, D'Aprix paid heed to emotions. He talked about relationships in the workplace, between colleagues, between line managers and their teams, about how people felt about the way they were treated, about the need to be heard and to be appreciated. He even talked about love, and while I remember pausing over this and questioning its relevance then, I revisited his work years later and, with more experience of life, bought into his thinking.

My observation both of client companies and as an employer is that a key differentiating factor between good and great places to work is the gift to create an arena where employees know they are valued and cared for, not only for the role they perform but also for who they are as people. This is an environment where people are positively emotional about the work they do, and the employers are positively emotional about them.

Creating a positive people culture

Having a positive people-focused culture is a huge differentiating factor in the workplace, and for some visionary leaders it is relatively simple to introduce and adopt. The challenge for some, however, is that adopting a people-based approach, like the PRIDE model, is more a philosophy than a process. Rather than rely on a set of complex systems and rules, leaders and influencers need to have an emotional conviction that people matter, and intention to show this in action at all times. Richard Branson writes fluently about this in *The Virgin Way*[5] and other publications, and it's a way that makes absolute sense to me. As an employer, if you want people to be passionate about your brand then you'd better be convincingly passionate about people.

A company culture is seen in the most basic examples of human interaction – for example in your own and your employees' manners, whether people speak to each other when they arrive at work. Leaders and line managers set the tone for the team and the wider culture, but everyone holds the power to support or threaten a culture. Not everything can be done by introducing and imposing rules.

It is a universal truth that if you are polite to your teams, the vast majority of people will be polite to you. They will also be polite to each other and your customers. Take interest in people's personal motivations and success and they will take interest in the organisation's. We are social animals. We like to be liked, valued and respected, and to work with people who show some interest in us and in our views.

An organisation that insists that managers at all levels take an interest in their teams is one that will create a culture of care, and as a result is more likely to drive collective responsibility for each other and a shared goal. The culture you create has far-reaching consequences for your employees and manifests itself to customers too.

Some employees have the luxury of working in close-knit teams with great management and camaraderie, sharing the same workspace and experiences that build familiarity and confidence. When things go well, they share the glory. When there are problems or snags, they can discuss and find solutions together.

Countless others, however, are working in more remote situations, away from a central office, and very often in customer-facing roles. Their employers require them to deliver the organisation's products or services and at the same time be fairly low-maintenance in terms of day-to-day contact and management. This demands a certain level of maturity, self-motivation and flexibility, as they need to deal with everyday demands and mishaps at work and think on their feet. Those employees need to know, just as much as any office-based staff, that they matter and belong. So it is essential that you provide them with a personal contact who cares, not only about task-related issues but also for them as individuals. Sadly, this common-sense requirement is not the norm in the UK workforce, and in some companies it is the exception.

The business case for a culture change

Taking an interest in your employees that reaches beyond the transactional work-for-pay contract is, in my opinion, non-negotiable in any successful organisation, yet it does not mean being soft.

From our client experience, organisational cultures are quite diverse. They spawn different processes and personalities, and they can be negative. Some feed on competition and division and others breed ignorance and disrespect. Generally, these are the ones that are suffering from poor performance and have approached us to support a change.

It hasn't always been easy to introduce the concept of care to those harder, more logical clients, but we started by reasoning, by demonstrating why they should care. We took them through the business case for employee motivation, the positive impact that harmonious employee relationships exert on business and team performance. We gave them the rationale for adding an emotional dimension to their role and to their colleagues' roles. We could not necessarily create respect but, even to the cynical, we have proved its value.

The sense of belonging that people feel with a brand or company is a key emotional factor in employee engagement, and that entails cementing connections with people who share common values and interests. People spend as much of their lives at work as they do with their friends and families, so it makes sense that our place of work becomes a place where we need to feel some cultural fit, and even ease. From the moment a newcomer joins you, they pick up the vibes. They want to feel at home, and if the culture resonates they will emulate it. If it doesn't, they may adapt, but they may also struggle against the norm, and this absorbs energy they would be better spending on their job. Most employee-engagement survey specialists will agree that emotions such as feeling secure, having a friend at work and sharing values with the people you work with are the chief emotional keys to engagement.

Employees in organisations with no sign of caring management often claim that they feel a stronger relationship with (and hence greater responsibility to) their customers than they do to their own bosses or their own brand. And if they believe their employer does not care, their whole contractual relationship is vulnerable.

Follow the leader?

Most companies that set out to define their culture tend to do so in a top-down way, starting with a project team working for the board or HR function to investigate their values as an organisation and how these fit their overall purpose and business strategy. If they are a new company, they may think about the kind of organisation they wish to be; if an established company, whether they need their culture to adapt or change. They may think about implementing that culture through a system that starts with a definition of leadership qualities and plays out through processes and procedures.

While that is a fairly logical first step, in order to take root the definition of culture needs to encompass the competencies and behavioural norms that people display throughout the organisation, from reception desk to CEO and every stage between. If a company has grown to thousands of people without defining culture, then you can't view it in a vacuum. Rather, you need to start with a realistic picture of how things are done, and then map that against how you want it to be. Creating or changing a culture is a multidimensional process.

Good and bad experiences crop up almost every day, and what draws the line between success and failure is often not what happens at work, but the way that it happens. And that depends on the behaviour of the leadership team, managers and colleagues. A lot has been written about the influence of the CEO and leadership team, both in determining the culture of the organisation and in signalling it in the employer brand. Simon Barrow believes that, while HR and internal communications are seen as specialists with employer-brand responsibility, 'the substance of an employer brand is created by the top team and in particular the CEO'.[6] I would argue that while you can't maintain the inner truth of a great reputation without the CEO and senior leadership, it is wrong to leave it to them to lead in isolation.

The role of the line manager

The larger and more complex an organisation, the more distributed the leadership is, and that puts the enacting of your culture, values and employee experience firmly in the hands of a distributed management team. As with so many aspects of successful business implementation, the linchpin between the strategic intent and the individual employee experience is the line manager.

Every one of us, at some point or another, has had a boss. Think about the best and worst you have had in your career. Think about how that made a difference, good or bad, to your experience of your job. And if you worked in a team, think how that boss influenced other people's mood, their commitment and productivity. I think about the managers I have worked for and I can still feel the physical and emotional highs and lows – the pleasure of being motivated and the pain of being humiliated. And I bet you have your own moments as well. Multiply that impact by the thousands of moments we have in our working lives and the thousands of people that are managed in your organisation, and you start to realise the importance of the individual. If you are CEO of an SME, you have the luxury of impacting the lives of every single one of your staff, and if you are good at your job your behaviour will have a positive impact. However, as CEO of a large organisation, you can certainly set an example, but then you have to rely on tens or hundreds of others to deliver a decent employee experience.

Your brand reputation relies on the integrity of your managers. Every day of the week, line-manager behaviour impacts the way your business runs and the way your employees feel. It also affects the behaviour of others. Knowing the type of behaviour you want to see in your organisation will determine the type of people you employ and promote, so this should not be left to chance.

Line managers have the potential to make or break your reputation with your customers, and likewise your employee's experience at work. They, more than anyone else, connect the 'what you do', as an organisation, with the 'how you do it'. As such, they are at the centre of your business relationships and the embodiment of your employer brand.

In conclusion, entrepreneurs don't generally start out in life with the ambition to employ people. They start businesses with a great idea and the drive to achieve it. But demand for the really good ideas grows, and in order to meet it entrepreneurs become the employers of thousands. Inspirational characters like Richard Branson, Larry Page, Steve Jobs or Jamie Oliver have become the business names of the century. They have succeeded partly by having great ideas and through creative brilliance, but equally through developing a brand proposition externally and internally that inspires others to work for them.

Doubtless, people get behind organisations when they have a sense of purpose and good reputation that they feel personally and that they share with their colleagues. They also need a good fair deal, and that includes a suite of tangible and intangible benefits, from pay and working conditions to feedback and development opportunities, where they are given encouragement and guidance. Sustainable success comes where their expectations are reinforced

WHAT DOES A GOOD LINE MANAGER LOOK LIKE?

A line manager is pivotal in the employee's relationship with their organisation. The best line managers I have known among my clients have these two distinct perspectives: on the one hand, they understand the business they are in and want to deliver great products and services to their customers; on the other, they are completely aware of what it takes to achieve results and motivate their teams to be the best they can be. Without exception, what they also share is an unshakable respect for people and the aim to achieve the best outcomes for all parties. From my experience, this is what good line managers in high-performing organisations generally look like:

- They are respectful and have a great sense of fairness
- They are self-motivated and able to motivate others
- They are clear communicators, able to give direction and clear instructions
- They are inclusive, yet decisive
- They are able to listen, consult with others, moderate, negotiate and reach decisions
- They give and receive feedback and act upon it
- They delegate tasks but maintain personal responsibility for team effort
- They praise, challenge and coach
- They are role models and advocates of the business
- They are committed to the team and relish its success

In the Action Plan for Integrity, we explore typical scenarios where line-manager behaviour can impact the employee experience of work.

by the personal experience of work and organisations deliver real integrity of their brand.

People and management practices, the employee journey, communication styles and company culture are all elements that put real meat on the bones of an employee value proposition. When an employee feels positive about the reality of what their job entails, how things are done and how they are treated, they will begin to decide whether they like what they see, how far they are prepared to become true ambassadors of the brand, and whether their role in the organisation holds some future for them.

Action Plan for Integrity: Making the inner truth of your organisation live up to employee expectation

You may find yourself in a company with great purpose and direction, where the external corporate reputation is good, but your people are not fully empowered and motivated as individuals. New recruits seem to arrive enthusiastic, but then they falter; they do not seem to 'give their all'. You may sense that managers do not make good decisions on their own; they rely too much on a top-down culture. You might therefore look at aspects of the brand's Integrity.

This part of the PRIDE approach is another mapping exercise, requiring you to put the employee experience to the test through walking in your employees' shoes and visualising the real experience they feel in your workplace to help you set targets and aspirations for the ideal desired change. It ends with the suggestion of a support mechanism enabling managers and influencers to develop great management style that will ensure the continuation of a positive, people-based culture in the organisation.

Map a typical week of life at work

It is individual behaviour that creates employee experience, whether good or bad. The approach here is to look at a typical week in the life of any employee and explore some of the moments where you as a colleague, line manager or boss could have a positive or negative influence. You can do this alone, or in teams with colleagues of different levels. The idea is to create a list of regular scenarios and discuss how they are currently happening and how they might work out more productively or more positively. Keep it impersonal: this is not the time to criticise or blame individuals. But allow discussion using real examples of how people feel about life at work, and how they would like to improve their experiences.

I'd like to thank my friend and client Jack Winters, formerly head of Corporate Internal Communications at Siemens UK, who has been both a manager and managed, for his contributions to this section. No list of events can be exhaustive, but I hope these examples of daily occurrences will demonstrate just how many opportunities we all have to make a positive or negative impact on the experience of those around us.

1. That Monday morning feeling – make it a good one

Picture the scene: you go to a party on your own, you walk into the party, everyone else is already there, talking to each other. Version 1: nobody looks towards you, nobody makes eye contact; you just shuffle in and work out how you can get into a conversation. Version 2: the host stands by the door, chatting to someone, she breaks off, says hello, welcomes you in and introduces you to the person she was chatting to. As a line manager, you are the host at the party, and it is up to you to welcome your guests. At best, people are coming to work well, motivated and happy or reasonably happy about being there. It is your job to keep the mood positive and upbeat. But everyone knows what it's like to come to work tired, a bit fed up, even hung over after a few days off. You, as a line manager, can never, ever show it. On the contrary, you need to conquer your own and counter anyone else's Monday morning feeling with a cheerful welcome. Of course, the party atmosphere is not created solely by the host, but he/she plays a very significant role in making it happen.

WHAT BAD LOOKS LIKE: THE GREETINGS OF
MICRO-MANAGERS

Working in a busy communications team supporting a big operational business can be really great. The environment, the urgency of delivery and the team spirit really makes you feel like you're playing your part.

Our new communications director was not the warmest of people – quite dismissive of others' views and strongly opinionated – people didn't warm to her easily. She advised us one day she had recruited a new internal communications director – someone who had worked for her previously. Her style was quite odd too – at an operational managers' communication project team meeting she attended in her first few weeks, she dismissed their work of the past six months, suggesting she knew better. Clearly she didn't. Previously we were well managed and felt motivated and enabled to do a good job. The new communications management style was very different – everything we did had to be approved by her. She worked very long hours, often starting before 7 a.m., and was always the last to leave. She rarely took holidays either. She would make decisions, without consulting the team. She rarely involved us and steamed ahead with her plans.

Business directors found her style quite strange, but because her boss sat on the company board and clearly stood by her working style (as she was the same), we were stuck. Our team engagement score was the lowest in the HQ services functions. We did wonder what culture must have existed where they worked before. In fact, most mornings the director of communications would come into the full office and only say good morning out loud to her internal communications director, ignoring the rest of us. Great leadership style in action! You can imagine the published company values and target behaviours become totally irrelevant when working for leaders like this. (JW)

2. Get to know your colleagues

Simple good manners and interpersonal skills make a huge difference to a working culture. My own experience at the advertising agency Yellowhammer was characterised by the passion for creativity and customer service that was demonstrated by all of the board and senior people, and a real commitment to sharing responsibility and accountability with the younger members of staff. My boss trained me in account-management practices that became real anchors in my career, and I have handed those on to my own teams ever since.

What really drove me to contribute was that both the founders, Jon Summerill and Jeremy Pemberton, created a culture that was full of lively, open discussion, whatever your level. Jon was at least 6' 4" tall, so it was quite a challenge to make eye contact, but he would make it a lot easier by planting himself on the edge of your desk to have a chat. I remember being asked what I thought about clients, their campaigns, other agencies, and it made me feel part of the team, much more important than I had felt in previous junior roles. He would also listen – something of a rarity in an agency head – and I got the impression that what I said was being stowed in a massive mental filing cabinet of opinion that would not ever be forgotten. It made me feel that Jon cared about who I was, and that my opinion mattered. But it also made me think a bit harder about what I believed and what I said – which, as a young, outspoken account manager, was a really helpful lesson to learn.

3. Check in with your team on progress

Office, factory, warehouse environments have different operational patterns, but regular team meetings to start the week or huddles to start a work cycle are fairly common. The line manager needs to know how to set an agenda and run a team meeting.

Team meetings are good ways of checking in with your team on what they are doing, how are they doing against their plans or targets, and whether you need to do anything to help.

They can serve as a status update on projects and also be a chance for people to find out about each other's work or share problems and fixes. A manager should be helping their team to work out the best way to do things, to improve efficiencies or performance.

Employees often complain that their meetings with their managers are dysfunctional, confrontational or unproductive. Some feel they would rather just get on with their own job than discuss it with their manager, because they are criticised in front of others, told to change their priorities or given new tasks without explanation.

A good line manager makes sure their employees know what they are responsible for, when they need to deliver it and, if priorities change, what they can do to help them shift work around. Employees need to know how much freedom they have within their role and be given the encouragement to take responsibility for delivering. If a manager removes their ability to make decisions, that will quell any desire to show initiative and take ownership.

4. Create the environment to talk about your work

Line managers should create an environment where employees feel comfortable about speaking, asking questions, voicing opinion. How consensus and decisions are reached differs from company to company and from culture to culture. What is key to engagement, however, is being able to contribute, being listened to, and seeing that employees' ideas are acted upon. Knowing how that works in your company should be transparent to your employees.

A line manager needs to be able to communicate to and often on behalf of their teams, representing their opinions or interests to other people and feeding back the resulting decisions. If a company culture prevents sensible discussion, there is a danger that people will expect and accept instructions without understanding. This means they cannot explain decisions to other people or provide answers to questions. If line managers are equipped with the reasons for decisions, then they are much more likely to be able to explain them to others. Discussion also encourages a culture of ownership over ignorance, positive inquiry over acceptance, and is more likely to contribute to innovation on the status quo.

5. Kill off 'them and us' thinking

In recent years, there has been a huge amount of reporting on the benefits of the networked organisation, enhanced and accelerated by the advance of digital and social technologies in the workplace. In my experience, technology has certainly created some great opportunities, but irrespective of digital and social platforms, some company cultures are more conducive than others to working together.

The most meaningful collaboration occurs in cultures where positive attitudes and behaviours are encouraged and often rewarded. For example, from early days working with the DHL organisation, I felt it was one of the most operationally and culturally networked companies I had ever known, and that was long before the arrival of digital collaboration channels.

Twenty years on, I believe that putting up barriers between departments, silo thinking, is one of the most negative and destructive forces I have commonly observed, particularly in large and complex organisations. How people from different departments and functions approach cooperation and collaboration can have a major impact on productivity and effectiveness.

In negative cultures, employees can be pitched against each other, blaming each other for mistakes and failings, or simply not talk to each other. Everyone, whether leaders, the board, line managers or team members, can influence the prevailing culture, but it is worthwhile to work on leadership dynamics and inter-relationships to set the right attitude. Boards or management teams are made up of specialists who lead departments with their own targets and responsibilities, but to support overall organisational success, they should fully appreciate how their goals and activities relate to and impact those of other departments.

There are key relationships and interdependencies that need to be managed and then understood throughout the organisation, and these are vital factors in creating a culture of respect. As part of this process, leaders, managers, HR and communications specialists should work towards communicating why every department matters, what it contributes to the organisation's goals, and how departments should positively work together.

6. Share information with teams

When I first started working in the area of employee-opinion surveys I was astonished just how poorly many companies scored on what seemed the most basic of issues. One of those was how far employees have the facts they require to perform their role well. It shocks me to observe how many people feel inadequately informed, and it is a requirement that I always wanted to see observed, however challenging, in my own company.

Some arenas of work in which people are notoriously bad at sharing information are time-pressured workplaces; split-shift operational conditions; high-growth companies where numbers of employees are also soaring; remote teams who have infrequent face-to-face time with colleagues or a boss; places where managers are travelling a lot; 'need-to-know' cultures where there are legitimate confidentiality issues relating to certain information – sometimes this spreads into areas that do not warrant confidentiality; highly competitive workplaces where individual results win high rewards.

Employees in such working environments regularly report feeling left out of the loop on what is going on in their own company and their client companies, often because of laziness or oversight on the part of their managers. If you recognise any of these conditions you should make sure that you assign the responsibility, time and opportunities for managers to share essential information with their teams.

7. Giving feedback, saying thank you and dealing with issues

Is there anything as simple as saying thank you for a job well done? Showing and receiving appreciation for personal effort is wholly motivating, so it is well worth while to make it happen regularly at work. Managers have a key role to play here.

Outside the largest employers, I have met many people who have been promoted into roles where they supervise others and have never received formal training. It is important for company leaders to spell out how managers should manage, and to provide staff with the skills and techniques that fit the desired culture of the organisation. Managers should also receive training in how to evaluate people's work and deliver positive and negative feedback. They should create an environment where teams can discuss improvements or change productively and can tackle employee concerns in a timely and professional way.

There are countless other incidents that can happen in an employee's average week, such as: a complaint from a customer, a big presentation to a client, positive or negative conversations and meetings that can impact the mood and motivation of your employees. Gather those stories from your own and your team's experience and then listen to how those everyday events are handled. Decide how satisfactory that is, how well it reflects your desired culture, and how far the reputation you want to transmit to your external customers is also reflected in the inner truth of your organisation.

8. The Hundred Club: a platform for managers to share experiences

Working with some of the world's largest companies and best-known brands has been a privilege, and I have witnessed some sophisticated and established leadership-development schemes and management-skills training. While the provision of formal training is often a one-off or one-time event for new managers, what has differentiated truly high-performing companies is the ongoing effort that some organisations make to build a mutual

---

WHAT GOOD LOOKS LIKE: HIGH-PERFORMING
TEAM ENGAGEMENT

In a new role as a Technical Sales Engineer and with a boss who was known to be a hard taskmaster, I was a bit apprehensive. But I soon realised that he had a different management style – and in a good way. First, he held monthly sales team meetings, which were well structured and very participative. They included looking at new opportunities, such as new customers or the latest products to promote. We had some technical training, or speakers from HQ telling us about the latest business changes or marketing campaign. We would also hear from the more senior sales guys sharing insights that we could all learn from. The agenda required everyone to play their part, and the team could discuss their challenges or practise their presentation skills in a safe team environment. These meetings were jam-packed with information, brainstorming and sharing, which was very motivational.

Routinely each month, he would also spend a typical working day with each of us. This was coaching at its best. He would observe, support, show and give constructive feedback. Team meetings and scheduled one-to-ones aside, he would keep a check on us – we knew that. He would sometimes call you when you were driving home at night to arrange to meet the following day first thing. This enabled him to check that you were booking sufficient sales calls and performing as required. The possibility of getting that evening call encouraged each sales engineer to plan sales calls well in advance.

It was no accident this management approach made his team the highest-performing with lowest staff turnover. Yes, his style could appear tough to outsiders, but to me it was inspiring, team engagement at its best. (JW)

---

and shared responsibility for employee engagement. This is often supported by individual coaching in robust interpersonal and communications skills.

What I have learned from working with some of my clients is that a great leader, with effective managers, can have a hugely positive impact on literally hundreds of people, but that it takes a sustained effort. This led me to try and create a template or process that draws from best practice and can be replicated in any organisation to make good management a constant, rather than an occasional agenda item.

The concept I put forward is called The Hundred Club, where managers or those who are responsible for let's say, a hundred employees, are given a platform where they can meet and share experiences. In an organisation of 20,000 employees, the management community could comprise around two hundred people, who, in their day-to-day jobs, may rarely connect with one another. The platform can be both a virtual and real-life meeting point, where this influential group of people are invited to network with each other, to access and share information and to develop strategies for dealing with the real-life situations that occur in their workplaces.

The virtual platform can be built on the company intranet or stand alone on one of the many communications and collaboration software systems that are now available. Some content would be centrally sourced material, such as guidelines that are specific to what is expected of line managers in a particular company, how to access information on strategic goals, how to facilitate strategy briefings, how to communicate with teams and how to manage performance reviews.

But the greater potential value lies in content that is shared by the network itself, for example, generic research, articles or presentations that the managers have found useful in their roles, or specific stories of challenges they have faced in their own organisations. Topics that emerge on the platform can then be discussed in person at board meetings or team meetings so that more can be learned, or actions can be taken based on shared experiences. Real-life connections can also be made by holding events for managers to share both success stories on managing and motivating teams, and ideas on how to create positive cultures.

While the plethora of collaboration software has created an opportunity for greater connectivity at work, making it happen – whether digitally or in real-life – requires time, resource and an organisational culture that is supportive of sharing. Not every organisation will think they need The Hundred Club, but the larger your number of employees, the more dispersed your locations and the more complex your reporting lines, the greater the need is for line managers who know how to manage, are open to learning and are supported in their role.

How does Integrity fit into the PRIDE model?

Integrity is the inner truth of your organisation. It flows through the way you conduct your business, every process, every transaction, every day, in every location. The experience that your employees have at work should live up to the external reputation of your organisation. It should reflect your stated purpose and it should enable them to fulfil their own ambitions, now and in the future.

Your employees can be your strongest advocates or most vociferous critics, because they know whether your brand reputation has integrity. The quality of your products and services, the way you treat your customers, leadership behaviours, team dynamics, the culture of your organisation – all these can test the authenticity of your purpose statements and your reputation.

When employees get to know the truth about your organisation from the inside, and find that its reputation is authentic, they will take pride in delivering and sustaining it. On this foundation, they will seek further opportunities to develop with the organisation, they will care about its future direction and will contribute to its positive energy.

4
Direction

In June 1999 I was having lunch with an old colleague from my time at the American trade publishing house Jobson Publishing. He was a marketing consultant and his business had tripled in the previous year, and so I think he was probably paying for lunch. We had worked in the same sector for much of the 1980s, but I had been out of the UK for six years and there was a lot to catch up on.

Between 1992 and 1998, I had moved to two different countries, learned how to live and work in different cultures, had two or three jobs, given birth to our second and third children, and since returning from Brussels in 1998 I had been busy with some interesting consultancy work, sourced mainly from DHL contacts back in Brussels. He asked what I'd been doing for the last year. When I told him I'd moved house, had been picking up with my old networks and done some freelance copywriting, he looked me straight in the eye and said: 'Mmm. Sounds to me like you're just drifting.'

At the time I thought that he'd been a bit harsh. Because he wasn't that interested in family stuff, I'd not mentioned that my husband was still working in the Netherlands, and that I'd managed the house move back to the UK with three kids under six, more or less on my own. I thought about how much change I had dealt with since 1992 and the watershed year that was 1998: nothing in my life had felt less like drifting.

But his words stayed with me, and I began to think about what his comment really meant. To him it meant that I had been doing the same thing for a long time, that I had made no progress, that my professional life (and therefore 'I') had no direction. He was out of touch, knew nothing about juggling dual careers and family, and how challenging that is to manage day to day, but his words really bothered me and I didn't like the inferred criticism.

A sense of direction, of growing from one state to another, of moving towards a goal, is an essential factor that can drive personal motivation and effort. Being a freelancer or working for a global corporate may set the context, but the idea of progress has universal meaning. In the previous two chapters we have examined how the reputational promise of a company or brand can attract employees, spark their ambitions and raise their hopes and expectations; and how the integrity or reality of that promise is an essential condition in sustaining their positivity and motivation. We have looked at how companies can satisfy employees' needs through an honest and genuine reputation that lines up with business reality.

The concept of Direction is the next key component of the PRIDE model, and it can be tremendously powerful in cementing employee relationships with an organisation and commitment to a role. In this chapter I shall examine three distinct dimensions of direction and suggest how an organisation's leadership can be more successful when they apply the concept in its broadest sense.

The first dimension: organisational direction

When it comes to buying into an organisation's direction, there is a vast difference between working for a start-up and for a conglomerate, and I believe it makes good sense to learn from the experience of both and anything in between.

For 80 per cent of start-ups in their first year, there is only one direction, and that is up; every customer is a founder-friend, every day brings new challenges and every employee feels like a key player. The pace and mood are probably highly charged, highly demanding and highly personal, and in my experience start-ups that grow to

SMEs provide a great employee experience based on shared goals, shared values and shared success.

The statistics get tougher after year one, however, with one in three start-ups failing by year three and a further half of the remainder failing in years four to six.[1] The reasons for failing are wide and varied, with a fair few related to market fluctuations and a lack of basic financial management such as bad debts or cash flow. Also reported as significant factors are the loss of focus by the company leaders and the lack of a long-term plan or practical roadmap. A sense of direction, even in the smallest of the SME sector, is as relevant for investors, customers and suppliers who are looking for sustainable relationships and ROI as it is for employees. Keeping a goal in mind, then, and communicating it clearly and regularly, is a fundamental leadership responsibility.

Proximity and access to leadership in start-ups or SMEs often drives a greater employee understanding and commitment to future direction, but it is not a given. People assume that in a small team, face-to-face contact is a daily reality, but with so many companies being formed on virtual networks this is not always the case, and so leaders need to reserve time to communicate with their employees from day one. A statement of purpose, annual key targets and regular performance reviews provide employees with a necessary framework for their own behaviour and activity.

In my own experience, leading a highly driven, service-oriented agency, it was a challenge to protect the time and space for internal communication, but it was an essential part of our culture to share goals, current work, new ideas and financial results so that everyone knew what was going on and could contribute. Surprisingly, even in a communications agency, it took effort and process to maintain a communications culture, but it yielded solid results in terms of quality, involvement and performance.

This approach will readily scale up as the organisation grows, using some simple and structured processes that keep the whole team focused on the same direction and aware of their contribution to the group effort.

Looking at a spectrum of high-performing companies reveals a few common success factors. First, there has to be commitment to communication and engagement from the very top of the organisation. Think CEO as the Chief Engagement Office personified,[2] and think Richard Branson: a giant of the modern global brand who has truly modernised the concept of a corporate organisation. A self-made billionaire who runs his businesses from a Caribbean retreat, he still manages to be accessible, personable, and in touch with thousands of customers and employees.

Richard Branson has a few natural advantages, personal charisma being fairly high on the list, as well as a gift for putting people at their ease. Not everyone can be a Richard Branson, but everyone can learn from him. Speaking at the IOD Convention in 2013, the advice he offered to entrepreneurs and budding business leaders was: recruit people to your teams who are more skilled than you. In his case, being both a visionary and dyslexic, he needed advisers who were more detail-oriented and – in his words – 'more clever in an academic sense'. He was also clear about how to manage and engage teams: 'You have to make sure that teams get on with each other and that the people who lead look for the best. Criticise rarely. Care about them genuinely. If people want job-shares or flexibility, try to accommodate them. Treat people in a humane way and they will become your greatest advocates.'

Communication is a core competency in the Virgin organisation and everyone is expected to practise it. The company invests heavily in face-to-face events, away-days and rewards schemes to keep its employees thoroughly tuned in to the company ethos. Customer focus is like a religion, and customer-facing employees are expected to channel their intelligence into product and service development. The way Virgin create their employee communications is outstanding, creative and quirky, and fully in step with their external brand. When talking to their people, they exploit the most practical and pragmatic channels so as to grab attention and make impact.

Despite his current wealth, which has enabled him to invest in Virgin Galactic, the world's first passenger space-line that will get more people into space, Branson didn't start life with any more communications channels at his disposal than anyone else. He simply believed in a strong message and appointed teams with creative ideas who delivered a great employee experience. And when it comes to communications, that meant regular briefings, publications, websites, conferences, ideas schemes – and a management philosophy that allowed people to show their personalities at work.

Richard Branson isn't alone in talking the talk and walking the walk of an engaging leader, but his approach and the Virgin culture is still regarded as exceptional, and, in spite of Virgin's massive business success, somehow 'risky'. The more cautious among my readers will be thinking about the gap that exists between their company culture and Virgin's. I would rather they look at the similarities: how their business success relies on their customer; their customer relies on their products and services; and the quality, development and delivery of their products and services rely on their employees. I don't quite understand why Branson's books sell thousands of copies, his blogs get thousands of hits, and yet so few companies seem to take his advice. If more did, leaders everywhere would listen and talk to their employees, and the collective impact on employee engagement levels, financial performance and the economy in general would be enormous.

How can communications help?

Branson wisdom aside, there have been several studies in the last ten years to prove that stakeholder engagement is positively impacted by visible leadership that delivers knowledge of and confidence in an organisation's future direction.[3] For some it will provide opportunity, for others security, but the common result is increased effort, motivation, commitment and loyalty to the brand. According to David MacLeod, co-founder of Engage for Success:

each organisation will have employees who are central to the execution of the business strategy, and the attitudes of

103

these people can greatly affect the way they perform their jobs as well as their willingness to remain in their current employment. Visible, empowering leadership is key to providing a strong strategic narrative about the organisation, where it's come from and where it's going and how an individual can contribute. Employees need to have a clear line of sight between their job and the narrative, and understand where their work fits in.[4]

Companies share their future strategies to a varying degree depending on their sector, their competitive position and their culture; and in different channels, including live events, film, cascade packs and brochures. Annual or quarterly conferences full of plenaries, workshops and whiteboards take place for managers and teams to debate and deliver functional or local implementation plans. Global, cross-functional or dispersed teams work on open collaboration platforms to share knowledge and thinking on innovation and development. Whether actual or virtual, at any given time communications team are having sensible debates about how much to share with whom – and thousands of pounds are being spent on sharing the big picture or rolling out strategy.

While many accept the perceived wisdom of the value of line of sight, fewer leaders really understand the importance of content and style. Even though face-to-face communications are the preferred option of most employees for most information, communications professionals have a way to go to help leaders stage their communications in a face-to-face form that has relevance and meaning to its participants.

One reason for this is the lack of understanding among many company leaders of their employees' attitude and expectations. Taking the worst-case scenario, imagine that a strategy that has taken three months or more to design is to be delivered in a keynote speech at the start of a conference in about forty-five minutes. No advance reading has been circulated, as the strategy is under wraps; the audience has gathered from all over the world; a quarter of them have jet-lag and half are listening in their second language. The CEO has been tinkering with his slides up till the last minute and refused to rehearse. Sounds like a train crash waiting to happen? We have all witnessed these in our time, yet it is so easily avoided.

To convert this experience into effective communication, leaders need to work on style and substance – preferably the substance first. The substance is of course the content, the message that needs to be presented, communicated and understood. You need to settle what is 'the story'. Why does it matter? Does it change something? How does it relate to the past? How does it connect with what we know or do now? And how does it open a path towards our future? Creating what some call a strong strategic narrative is a key step towards communicating direction. It should make instant contact with the people who need to hear it.

Next comes knowledge of and respect for the participants' current opinion. Many presenters I have worked with, CEOs among them, will put a lot of thought into what they want to communicate before they really consider whom they are communicating with. The bigger the company and the steeper the hierarchical curve, the more challenging it is for leaders to stay in tune with employees, but they need to maintain real knowledge of their employees' concerns. It is a common but inexcusable criticism of leaders that they are out of touch; they should be positively 'in touch' and interested in who their employees are. A key role of HR and communication specialists is to create plenty of open lines of contact and encourage a mutually respectful culture, where leaders listen and employees have the confidence to speak.

An environment where leaders understand their employees and employees feel that their voice is heard will conduce to effective communications. That applies both for day-to-day operational communications and for conveying a strategic narrative. It is far easier to tell a story in the right way when you know the people you are talking to. You can adopt the right tone, give more relevant examples, and explain the reasons and impacts of what you are communicating in terms that really mean something.

Another common failing of strategic communication is that leaders try to deliver it in a single 'hit' without due preparation time, but also without follow-up. It is fairly unusual for people to retain 100 per cent of any piece of communication they receive, so leaders should make regular and repeated reference to their organisational direction.

The typical hierarchy of operational companies has created a traditional top-down model of cascade communication that is entrenched in the attitudes and mindsets of some company leaders. Changing workplace dynamics and new communications practices are often thrown up as reasons to move away from the cascade, but even in the most traditional working cultures, one-way has rarely been effective. Rather, a leadership vision, a company strategy or any employee communications is a process of listening and debate as much as it is presenting and delivering.

Nevertheless, while company leaders and the best communicators can set and share the direction of the company in a way that comes through to their employees, this alone is not enough to drive engagement behind it. The second dimension of direction looks at the individual employee in terms of their personal engagement with the company.

The second dimension: job-specific direction

If you are sitting in a large organisation with multiple tiers, sites and functions, understanding the dynamics of each and every employee's relationship with their job might seem like an impossible task. Yet it is exactly what effective company managers and team leaders claim makes the tangible difference between average and high-performing teams.

Leaders need to stop thinking of all their employees as a single mass and start regarding them as a collection of smaller, distinct groups, teams or shifts of people who come together every day to perform certain roles and tasks. The bigger the overall number of employees, the more there are of those smaller communities, but every single one is important: it is the dynamics of each that will most affect an individual employee's performance.

All companies have data that relate to their own performance – whether in terms of revenue, profitability, productivity or employee opinion – which should be traceable to individual sites or teams. While each measure taken on its own provides a single dimension or headline score, much insight can emerge from looking at the correlations between them and delving deeper into the areas of exception. Where the business seems to be going really well in one dimension, what are the causes? Where certain metrics keep on falling short, what are the consequences? I would claim with some certainty that the positive attitude of the leadership would count highly in impacting employee commitment, and that positive attitude includes a healthy interest in individual team members.

If a company is too big for a CEO or senior leader to know every community, then the role of the line manager, again, comes sharply into focus and the duties of managing people have to be shared. In order for line managers or supervisors to meet this responsibility, they have to be able to spread the leadership vision and implement a plan, but they also need to really know their teams and understand how connected their employees feel to the role they play and the company that is paying their salaries. This is an essential factor in building and maintaining team spirit and personal motivation, and it needs time and effort and a certain emotional intelligence, but given the application and commitment it can be achieved.

When you start to look really closely at the individuals within an organisation, you will discover that not every employee is at the same stage of their relationship with the company, or feeling the same commitment. From new recruits to long-termers, according to the depth of their relationship, these stages differ widely. There will be high-performers, self-starters, leaders and followers, and all of them at varying phases of their relationship with their employer and with their jobs.

As mentioned earlier, Roger D'Aprix famously pointed out how all too often leaders will present their future visions and strategies regardless of the basic state of mind of their employees. If they cared to find out, they would know whether the organisation's future agenda would or would not appeal to their employees.

Achieving commitment to a shared vision and a desire to make a contribution to a company's success comes with sound management that recognises the motivations of employees. In order to maintain that commitment, employees need to feel they have their basic needs fulfilled and that they are valued members of the team. But in order to really fly, the job has to be in tune with the employee's sense of personal direction at that time. Let's take a look at when and how that occurs, and what leaders and managers can do to bring all three dimensions together.

The third dimension: personal direction

I believe that there is a huge spectrum of individual ability, and indeed desire, to set one's own direction. Some people are born with the aspiration to become doctors or teachers, others to act or to paint. Some are conditioned to follow a path of professional qualification; others have a vocation. Young people all over the world, for reasons unknown, will decide to follow in their parents' professional footsteps, others will roundly reject them. There are natural leaders and natural followers in all walks of life, people who are looking for a mission themselves or those who would rather draw inspiration from others. How individuals end up in a particular professional environment still depends largely on fate. Happily, most of us survive, adapting to different rules throughout our working lives, acquiring various skills and group behaviours along the way.

The workplace can feel like a melting pot of unnatural, learned and acquired behaviours, where at times everyone but you seems to know the rules, or at others you can branch out, be bold and make up your own. Most people settle for the experience of something in between, but I believe the most fulfilling experiences, and the instances of highest engagement, occur when employees find themselves in an inclusive working culture, where they feel they simply fit in and can be themselves.

Being oneself at work means being seen for who one is, and so leaders, again, need to open up to learning about whom they have on their teams. In any group of employees, there will be people who are at different life stages, with more or less to learn and likewise to give, and yet all of them have the potential to be highly motivated in their role and highly engaged in the future of the organisation.

In his book *The 7 Habits of Highly Effective People*,[5] Stephen Covey talks about a natural cycle of dependence, independence and interdependence that occurs through our lives from childhood to maturity. When it comes to team dynamics, it helps to work out where people are on that cycle of behaviour and how their personal ambitions can be linked to their professional performance. There are also a few considerations to be made about the changing patterns of engagement drivers across different ages and life stages.

For example, there are big differences in perspective between those looking at a job at the start of their careers, and those who have worked for ten, twenty, thirty years; between people whose lives are at a crossroads and those who have multiple dependants. In every company there will be people who are seeking to broaden their skills and to learn, and others who are looking to make a contribution or for new challenges; there will be people with the time and energy to make positive choices, and others who are time-poor and have put their personal ambition temporarily on hold to accept a job that is containable. There may be others who, for a whole host of personal reasons, are at this point in their careers apparently 'drifting'. None of those considerations in themselves should be seen as a limiting factor to being a high performer in a particular role, or to putting one's full weight behind a company direction.

Appreciating a balanced team means grasping the benefits of difference. When a leader creates such a culture of mutual respect it enables everyone to recognise the value of their own and other people's contribution to a common cause. While consulting some of the world's largest employers on employee-engagement approaches over the last twelve years, I have also had to put some of these theories to the test as an employer. I have certainly felt the pleasure of a team working with a common ambition, as well as the pain when the goals of the company no longer match an individual's perspective. I have experienced the value of diversity at first hand, and value generational and personal aspirational differences. It has led me to adopt an attitude of constantly learning from others, and to appreciate that the future perspective of a twenty-something is different from that of a fifty-something.

To conclude, my belief is that for an employee to truly fly in an organisation calls for a fusion, or 'fit', of three dimensions:

- knowledge and confidence in the future of the company;
- opportunity to contribute that drives individual commitment to the current job;
- awareness and accommodation of the individual's personal situation.

An organisation's leadership has it in its power to tap into all of those motivations. Communications professionals can help their leaders take the dimensions, work on their skills and tools to deliver both the directional lead and the employee engagement cycle, and weigh up the value of true diversity in the workplace.

Going back to my critical friend from 1999, however irritating he was at the time, I have to admit that I do owe him a favour. Over the next year or so, with my family much more settled and my husband back in the UK, I started to consider what I wanted to achieve next in my work-life. I soon stopped 'drifting' as a freelance copywriter and made some important decisions that set my own direction: as a consequence, I found some like-minded people, founded an agency and set off on the path that eventually led to PRIDE.

Action Plan for Direction: How to make people feel confident in the future of their organisation and their role within it

You may be working in a successful, customer-focused business, which is expanding. Its founders still run it, but they recently raised outside funding and made acquisitions. There are new pressures to report to the investors and also to integrate the acquired employees into the company. The leadership team is excited by the future growth potential but is spending less time with the day-to-day business, and employees are unsure of their future and where they fit. Questions are being asked about future direction.

This is a commonplace scenario for high-growth and lean companies, where all the decisions and leadership tend to rest with a small number of people who assume that everyone knows what the strategy is.

Nevertheless, in all organisations irrespective of size, Direction needs to be voiced and communicated regularly, to help people feel more connection with the leadership, and possibly with each other. The PRIDE solution is for the leadership team to create a strong strategic narrative and enlist a wider team in order to implement and communicate it.

1. Establish a common 'summary' view of the company strategy

If you are not the creator of the company strategy, then you need to talk to the person who is, usually the CEO, or a representative of the leadership team. It helps to have an exploratory session face to face with the people/person responsible for creating the strategy, so that you hear how they articulate it. It may be a short statement, or it may be a fully documented strategy paper, but it should be possible for the owners of the strategy to explain it simply. Have them describe the current performance of the organisation, its position in its sector marketplace and its long-term goals. You should establish at this point whether the organisation is in a stable position, whether the market is growing or shrinking, whether there are major changes on the horizon, and how far the strategy is already communicated/understood in the organisation.

When I set to work with executives on a strategy story, I start by getting a view from them on what is already in the public domain. I often ask them to imagine they are being interviewed for a high-quality business magazine and want it to result in a positive feature, one that encourages people to invest in, or maybe seek employment with the organisation. The starting points are:

- who is the organisation and what does it do?
- who are the main stakeholders?
- what is their experience?
- how is the strategy guiding the organisation to meet their needs in the future?

This provides context that will help the narrative, moving on to the last question, which deals with their view of the organisation's direction.

Leaders rarely spend as much time communicating strategy as they need to, and, when they do, they are often outwardly focused towards investors and customers. They need to think about telling the strategy story internally as well, with the same vision and substance, but in a way that makes sense to the people delivering on it.

2. Explore the strategy

The lack of a clearly stated strategic direction is surprisingly commonplace. The people who are responsible for it are often caught up in the details, or responsible for just one part, and apt to lose sight of the bigger picture or the desired end. They may not perceive why it matters to communicate it, they may not plan to share it, and will be unaware that people on the staff turn up for work and have no idea where the company is going. On the other hand, you may find that the strategy is embedded in the organisation, and there is a fair knowledge of the direction of travel, but employees have no chance to discuss it, or contribute to future thinking.

Exploring the strategic direction means finding out about the different aspects of the organisation's activity, who has charge of what, who delivers the present and who turns an eye to the future. How much of the future strategy has been translated into implementation plans, with budgets, resources and deadlines, and how much is a high-level vision? How far can people challenge the strategy? How far do current targets and goals promote it? Do they understand where they fit? Is there that precious line of sight between what an individual is doing in their job and where the organisation is supposed to be heading? Casting people in the strategy story shows where it has come from and how it relies on participation. This will broaden its appeal and give everyone more sense of what lies ahead.

3. The big picture, not the whole picture
There is a lot of debate about how much the average employee wants to know about the company, in terms of its performance or future strategy. I believe the story should be created with a view to appealing to a wide employee population, anticipating positive interest, rather than being exclusive to a few decision-makers and influencers and dismissing the rest as uncaring or uninterested.

Nevertheless, it is smarter still to support this approach with fact and take the time to understand the different needs of your employees before embarking on communications.

It is important for everyone to have at least a common understanding of the core meaning of the strategy, and where it will take the whole organisation, but it is rarely necessary or productive for everyone to know everything. You can make it clear that a future strategy has many parts and they all fit together, without overloading people with too much detail.

4. Make it relevant, use the right language and the right channels
When people work for a start-up or an SME, they are likely to know and recognise their leadership team. In large organisations,

this simply doesn't happen, and there is often a hierarchical and communications gap between the people who have determined the future direction and the people who will need to implement or follow it.

When you start to deliver a strategic narrative, you have an opportunity to present the people who have worked on it, and allow them to tell the story. You also have a duty to communicate it in a way that means something to the recipients. The core messages need to be consistent and clear, but the story must also be told in terms that everyone will understand – and that means in different words for different levels and in different languages for different nationalities. Many employees complain about inaccessible business jargon or 'corporate speak' that clouds any real meaning, so try to make sure that people can really hear what you are saying. One way to test this is to ask the question: 'Could you share this story with others?'

Your strategic narrative will need to be delivered in different channels to suit different people. Some will need the words, others will understand more from pictures, infographics and videos. The more creatively you tell your story, the more people will remember, relate to and repeat it.

5. It's not all about telling

Of course, telling the story is also only part of the process. The whole idea that employees are simply 'an audience' to be performed to, or talked at, is demeaning. Employees are the main players in an organisation, they are the pilots not the passengers, the surgeons not the patients, and the company strategy is really *their* strategy too. It is important that employees should be able to discuss the strategy and work out ways to contribute. One of my former clients used to say that a big idea (be it a vision or a transformation) is no use unless it is broken up into lots of smaller operations. People need to know what they have to do and have the time and the resources to do it. Again, a large company needs more than the leadership team to achieve a desired direction, and so it relies on line managers to work with teams to put plans into action. Giving your employees a voice at any level of your communications makes for a more inclusive and collaborative culture. Giving them the opportunity to take part in developing their own plans is a smart way to gain their creative contribution and commitment.

6. Feed back on progress

Whenever and however you choose to signal your organisation's direction, make sure that it is not a single event or announcement with no follow-up. Your people need to know whether the organisation is being successful and how it is performing against its stated objectives. Having confidence in the future requires evidence of success in the present. Set up regular reports on how the organisation is doing and give employees feedback on how their efforts contribute to collective outcomes. There will be times when the strategic direction needs to be reinforced, and others when it needs to be changed. Those who have real understanding and involvement in their company's direction are much more likely to respond positively and adapt to change.

7. Make it personal

In line with the other elements of PRIDE, goals for development should also have a personal perspective, so when you are thinking about your company's future, give thought to creating a scheme whereby individuals can progress in your organisation and influence their own future. All employees should understand what it takes to succeed in your organisation, how their current skill set meets its expectations, and see room for personal growth or development. Leaders need to set the competency framework for their organisation, but also to view their staff as individuals. Who is able and ready to move from one job to another? What will enable them to fulfil future tasks? Which people wish to stay where they are, and who is seeking a change of direction? Performance management and encouraging personal development is very much part of an overall management philosophy covered in the Integrity module, but bear in mind too that employee confidence in their own, as well as the organisation's, direction has a telling impact on achieving pride.

How does Direction fit into the PRIDE model?

People and organisations rarely stand still. Circumstances change, and so do personal ambitions and aspirations, market forces and customer needs. Employees invest time and energy in their work, and most of them want to use their talents and expand their skills. Likewise, in order to survive and thrive in a dynamic, competitive world, businesses need to think differently, develop new products, open new markets. They need to establish future business strategies, and to see their employees fired up and motivated to make it happen.

Direction extends the life of the PRIDE model and strengthens the ties that people develop with their work. A sense of direction and understanding of the value of personal involvement are positive motivational factors. Organisations that establish and communicate future strategies set high expectations both external and internal. They build not only consumer but also employee confidence, and create energy and excitement about the future.

5
Energy

There are times when the energy in a room is so strong that you can almost touch it.

You can certainly feel it in the moment, and now and then its impact lives on. In 2016, when the Italian tenor Andrea Bocelli walked onto the stage at London's 02 Arena to perform to an audience of 16,500 people – the largest ever in the venue's history – the mood was so charged with anticipation that his mere arrival brought tears to my eyes. When he started to sing, my heart set to pounding, and days after the performance I was still on an emotional high from sharing so deep an emotional experience with so many people.

Similarly, I can still remember the raw energy radiating from the actor Mark Rylance in the stage play *Jerusalem* more than five years ago, when he created a character full of mischief and melancholy that held the audience in a state of hypertension for the entire three-hour performance. People leaving the theatre that night seemed to be deep in conversation or thought, wrestling with the issues he had portrayed. Taking part in an event with thousands of people focused on the same activity made it another uplifting experience.

I am also energised by hearing individuals sharing their thinking or creativity in a more personal way that touches my spirit. At every TED event I have ever attended I have been educated, shocked, intrigued by different speakers, but ultimately inspired to think differently by hearing outstanding people telling their stories. Others will recall their own heroes, or sporting events, or festivals and challenges that project a thrilling moment or surge of energy that is outside the norm or the typical day. Whether you feel it in places, occasions, individuals or shared experience, energy is a vital part of life that creates a reaction or feeds a passion, and connects you with your deeper emotions.

Can we aspire to create such moments at work? I think so. An energetic workplace will attract customers and employees alike; it will encourage a more positive culture and sustain employees' passion to deliver high performance. It will feel like a more driven, thrilling, fun and successful place to be. And I can cite several examples of shops, restaurants, holidays, even classrooms and clinics, where a positive energy creates an atmosphere that *makes* the experience.

Energy will feed and be fed by individual motivation, participation, performance and resilience. It heartens others in good times, and in bad. It will enable and inspire employees to step up their efforts, solve problems, conquer difficulties, or simply be more supportive colleagues.

In chapter 5 of the PRIDE model, I examine the factors in work that can tip the scale between a passive and an energetic culture, a reactive and a proactive attitude, and a satisfied and an excited employee. In three sections focusing on body, mind and soul, I will look at how to create a palpable buzz that is good for your organisation and for the people that work there.

A healthy body: physical environment and workplace culture

As discussed in the earlier chapters, organisational culture grows from a number of sources, from the declared purpose and goals, through processes and systems, to the quality and value of the products and services you provide. Culture is also most strongly expressed and demonstrated in the values and behaviours of the people who lead and those who deliver. The workplace environment should not only reflect your brand and support your outside reputation, it should also uphold its integrity in the daily experience of your employees. It should provide a place that supports your employees to deliver the right results for your organisation and at the same time to nourish and renew their physical energy.

Across all sectors of work, layout, technology, equipment, furniture and lighting are key details that sway employee motivation and workplace energy. All environments are governed by specific operational requirements and processes of work, but they should also make room for employee preferences on where and how they interact, what feeds their physical energy, and how much control they have over their surroundings for different tasks. No matter what the operational factors that rule your workplace infrastructure, the way you personalise your workspace is a strong indicator of your company's culture.

A look inside high-performing companies such as Unilever, Diageo and Google teaches us how to create workplaces that not only promote their employees' goals in the most efficient way, but also give options to recharge their batteries, whether through moments of relaxation or through social interaction with other colleagues. Here, workspaces are designed for different types of activity, with quiet booths, breakout rooms, whiteboard walls and playful relaxation areas.

Energy also flows with the freedom to show initiative and take risks. Employees have clear goals and accountabilities within teams, they give and receive regular feedback from managers and peers, but they also enjoy great personal autonomy. They have flexibility and choice about where and how they work, they are encouraged to move around, interact with others, and not be tied to a specific desk or traditional meeting format. They are invited to take part in several projects at a time and to cross-fertilise ideas in different physical workspaces and digital platforms.

Among the tech giants, such as Apple and Google, different cultures of collaboration and innovation have emerged. Nonetheless, employees who have known both cultures report common factors that include respect for rational and fact-based argument, strong evidence of cultural diversity and respect for individual circumstances. Crucially, in their systems of working they sustain the discovery process by allowing time and energy for creative thinking and problem-solving to actually happen. Google, for example, allows employees to spend 20 per cent of their time on creative ideas that they are passionate about, and it comes as no surprise to find that they have delivered spectacular innovation and product development as a result.[1]

Not everyone is, or wants to be, like Google, and to introduce free thinking time and recreational play areas does not suit every corporate. Nevertheless, organisations should take some lessons from the innovators and find their own ways to nurture the physical energy in the workplace.

Employee wellbeing

Enlightened employers are not only thinking about the environment they create, they are also investing in the physical health and fitness of the people who join them. This is a two-way contract. Employers have a duty of care to protect the health of those who work for them, while they are at work. It is the employees' responsibility to maintain a level of fitness so as to do their jobs. Health goes beyond working hours, and while the personal choices we make to stay healthy at home are arguably our own affair, it is of mutual benefit if employers promote health and wellbeing as a lifestyle choice and employees stay healthier and fitter for longer. Furthermore, positive health management is also good for society and the economy.

This argument was reinforced in a report published in 2014 by the newly formed Public Health England (PHE),* which stated: 'The link between health and work is increasingly well understood: good quality work promotes better health, and a healthier workforce is a more productive one.' PHE's first policy statement named the

---

* A single agency founded in 2013 in the UK that assembles public health specialists from more than seventy organisations. Its mission is to protect and improve the nation's health and to address health inequalities through working with national and local government, the NHS, industry and the voluntary and community sector.

contribution of employers as one of the six game-changers to improving people's mental and physical health,[2] and in its first year it launched a set of national standards on workplace health, the Workplace Wellbeing Charter, which provides a roadmap for businesses wanting to improve the health and wellbeing of their staff.

Wellbeing policies, it advised, should complement existing legal regulations, operational health and safety guidelines, or any other work procedures that govern your sector, and they should be accessible to all employees. Typically, activation plans will include sections on working patterns, hygiene, hydration, diet, physical exercise, alcohol, drug and tobacco abuse policies, and access to therapies.

By law, all employees should take regular breaks, but different jobs cause different physical stresses and strains. Office-based employees can often fall into the habit of never moving from their desks; engrossed in their screens, they may spend long spells without refreshment. People in customer-facing roles, such as retail, transport or healthcare sectors, can be governed by specific rules about when and where to eat and drink. Unforeseen events or extensions to working hours can delay the occurrence of these breaks. Employees need special arrangements to be made for working in extreme temperature conditions or on long uninterrupted shifts (such as surgeons or theatre nurses).

Many employers now incorporate national campaigns into their wellbeing policies, such as the British Nutrition Foundation's Healthy Eating Week. This campaign sets five health challenges to UK workplaces to promote drinking plenty of water, having breakfast, eating five pieces of fruit and vegetables a day, getting active and trying something new. High-performing companies and corporate wellbeing specialists are going much further to provide a balanced, healthy diet to their people. UK award-winning corporate caterers Charlton House have pioneered nutrition at work through reformulating recipes to provide tasty meals that are lower in fat and salt, as well as assuring responsibly sized portions of foods within 500 calories per meal. It's not all about canteens, though. Organisations should also provide more healthy snacks and drinks in their vending machines, and replace biscuits with a fruit basket at other informal workplace gatherings.

Hand-in-hand with healthier diets go many schemes to introduce more physical activity to employees in and outside the workplace. Provision of onsite pedometers, exercise bikes and exercise classes are all examples of relatively low-cost and low-maintenance ways of encouraging wellbeing at work. Discounted gym membership, sports club vouchers, and walk or cycle to work schemes are also offered by many employers as part of flexible benefits and incentives to staff.

A report in the *Guardian* in 2015 pointed to a number of SMEs that were providing personal trainers and fitbit devices to encourage more exercise during the working day.[3] A case was also cited in Turkey where a public-sector department was allowing employees to arrive one hour later for work on one day each week, as long as that hour was spent on exercise.[4] Many companies also combine wellbeing activity with their external sponsorship or community engagement through open sporting events or charity challenges.

The Workplace Wellbeing Charter brought the topic into the mainstream for employers, and there is more and more information to digest on the topic. The charity C3 Collaborating for Health is an excellent source of best-practice and implementation advice for corporates, particularly in gauging communication and impact.

Most schemes include consulting with employees, education, regular advice and impact measurement. It is best to explain the context for wellbeing and not to patronise employees with shallow messages. 'Be honest about your motives, if you are interested in productivity, do not pretend that you are only interested in individual wellbeing, because you will be found out. Don't underestimate the amount your employees already know', they advise. 'And be ready to answer the questions "who are you to tell me to change?" and "where does your authority come from?"'

Among others, C3 present a growing body of evidence to show that organisations with smart wellbeing initiatives experience lower sickness rates, reduced employee turnover, higher productivity and employee engagement.[5] What leaders in the field also maintain, however, is that those organisations with smart wellbeing programmes are generally more resilient, and employees better equipped to adapt to change.

The Chartered Institute of Personnel and Development (CIPD) has gone as far as to say that wellbeing is a means of 'creating an environment to promote a state of contentment, which allows an employee to flourish and achieve their full potential for the benefit of themselves and their organisation'. The word 'contentment' makes the implicit link not only between health and productivity but also between health and happiness.

A healthy mind: mental health and happiness

This chapter, together with the earlier chapter on Integrity, has looked into several aspects of providing a good and healthy place to work. Simply the way employees are treated – on a human level – from day to day has tremendous impact on their physical wellbeing. Displaying respect for the individual is fundamental to mental health, too.

Let's start from the optimist's position that work has the potential to vastly enhance an individual's mental health. It can provide purpose, achievement, reward and a feeling of fulfilment. People who are putting their skills to good use, mastering challenges and developing their talents can be positively energised and engaged in their own and common goals. But this feel-good factor shouldn't be left to chance. I believe that in order to create a successful business, with employees capable of keeping up that effort, employers have a responsibility to protect and nourish their mental health and happiness as well.

Getting the basics right in terms of fair treatment, pay, working patterns and allocating workload is a good place to start. Significant work-related stress occurs in job roles that carry what analysts call high effort/low reward and high demand/low control. These are jobs where employees experience, for example, low pay, job insecurity, no prospects of promotion or little scope on decision-making. Senior people within the health service have lobbied for policies that ensure that jobs are fairly paid, work is fairly apportioned, and employees can control their schedules. They have had effect on negotiating minimum wages and introducing flexible working as a right for all employees, and these have been cited as a core contributor to mental health improvement. Yet all too often employees suffer at the hands of rogue managers, who make unreasonable demands to extend or reduce hours, give little notice for changes in shift pattern, or pay no heed to employees' out-of-hours commitments. When policy decisions are made at a high level, it is vital to implement them fairly across an organisation's functions and sites, and to give training to all managers with work-planning and people responsibilities so as to eliminate needless triggers of workplace stress.

Workplace stress is not confined to lower-paid or junior employees either, as other causes, such as exhaustion and burnout, claim victims across the economic spectrum. Lynda Gratton cites the advance of globalisation as a factor that has extended people's working day across time zones, and is draining their physical energy and resilience.[6] The constant pressure to deliver more for less during periods of flat economic growth has required most employees to show greater resilience than ever before in their working lives.

One of the negative consequences of digital innovation and the twenty-four-seven society is that work rarely stops when employees leave their workplace. While some would view constant connectivity as the huge upside of digital communications, others feel that such technology has wiped out boundaries between their work and their home lives.

Recent employee-health research points to galloping stress levels among senior executives, with three-quarters of respondents blaming mobile technology for creating a more stressful environment. Sixty per cent stated that their employers expect them to answer emails outside work hours, while a fifth said that 'switching off from work at home' is their biggest challenge in terms of looking after their health.[7] My view is that how people and companies manage connectivity and communications *outside* the workplace is another dimension of job flexibility and employee choice, and organisations should adopt specific policies on out-of-hours contact that respect the need for time and space to relax and recuperate.

Reacting to a high occurrence of conditions such as stress and burnout, early spenders on mental health programmes in the workplace have tended to come from the public sector, such as the NHS, social care and the prison service, and from private-sector areas like finance services and management consultancy. However, there is a growing trend towards more proactive spending by large employers, for example in the hi-tech, innovation and other professional services. Recognising that they live or die by the mental capability and agility of their workforce, and that some of their working habits are leading to mental health issues, forward-thinking organisations in these sectors have been keen to explore techniques for improving stress management and enhancing resilience.

Training for the mind

One pre-emptive technique for improving stress management and increasing resilience that has prospered in recent years is the practice of mindfulness, an ability to focus one's mind on the experience of the moment, in terms of inner thoughts and feelings, and their relation to the external environment. It is described by the UK's policy unit The Mindfulness Initiative as 'a human capability, like language acquisition' that trains practitioners to resist the mind's natural tendency to stray into past experience or future plans, and to pay greater heed to the present moment. While mindfulness training is often used by the medical profession to help those with depression, it is also being adopted proactively by people seeking new forms of personal development and improved mental wellbeing.

In 'Building the Case for Mindfulness in the Workplace,'[8] a collaboration of academics and UK companies such as BT, Ernst & Young, General Electric, HSBC and Jaguar Land Rover, research suggested that individuals who practise mindfulness develop greater awareness of their own and others' emotions, improve their ability to listen and respond more compassionately to conflict. Employees who practise mindfulness in the workplace also report improved concentration and decision-making and reduced stress. Leaders who had been trained in mindfulness also advanced the wellbeing of others, as employees reported greater satisfaction of their psychological needs, less emotional exhaustion, better work–life balance and better performance ratings.

This experience is echoed in the US, where technology leaders such as MIT Social Media Lab, Apple and Google were early champions of mindfulness in the workplace, and have promoted its benefits as improving powers of concentration, stress management and the quality of relationships. Google believes that it enhances listening and decision-making skills and teaches emotional intelligence, which helps with understanding colleagues' motivations. It also teaches people to be fully present in the moment, and leads to focus and clarity of thought.[9]

As the developed nations shift from industrial to knowledge economies, and measure 'human capital' in terms of 'mental capital', more companies are expected to follow their lead. Since organisations claim to view their people as their greatest assets, the prospect is that more effort will now go into caring for their minds, as well as their bodies, and the business case supports the investment.

Techniques such as mindfulness can have a positive impact not only on the mental energy of the individual but also on the organisational capacity for decision-making, creativity, innovation, resistance to challenge and resilience. It can also make the workplace a more pleasant, happier place to be, where individuals show more tolerance and mutual respect. As the Workplace Initiative confirms, mindfulness is 'supportive of a culture where relationships are valued'.

Working to your heart's content

Understanding of how to achieve happiness at work has been pioneered by the psychologist Mihaly Csikszentmihalyi, who identified a state of 'flow' that occurs when someone is so absorbed in what they are doing that nothing else seems to matter.[10] 'Flow occurs when you are really involved in creating something, so that you can't process anything else. You are doing something really well that requires a lot of concentration and are free from other concerns and worries.' He has specialised in the psychology of work and creativity, where people in flow are 'working to their heart's content' on stretching tasks and challenges that truly test their capabilities.

Companies that have introduced flow management have seen process, productivity and service-performance improvements, simply through rising emotional participation and engagement among their employees. It relies on managers finding out how their employees feel, what they enjoy doing, what they are good at, and then assigning people to the most appropriate tasks and giving them the chances to excel. Flow operates across multiple layers of organisational models, and has been found to occur in highly professional, skilled and semi-skilled workforces. It also positively impacts teams, where through 'flow contagion' groups of people feed off each other's positive involvement. Csikszentmihalyi wrote:

> Surgeons say that during a difficult operation they have the sensation that the entire operating team is a single organism, moved by the same purpose; they describe it as a 'ballet' in which the individual is subordinated to the group performance, and all involved share in a feeling of harmony and power.[11]

Feeding the healthy mind: ideas worth sharing

When you are running a company or managing a team, theories such as flow and workplace happiness do not just land in your lap, but are rewards for having an inquiring mind. In order to consult effectively with leaders and to develop techniques for my own business, I have sought prior inspiration from as many external sources as possible.

To be insightful and creative, I believe it is essential to broaden as much as to deepen your fields of influence and learning, drawing inspiration from a wealth of sources and a wide network of thinkers with different passions, styles and experiences of working environments. I would particularly encourage anyone who spends a long time in the same organisation or environment to maintain wide connections on the outside to feed back different perspectives and contexts.

One of the most famous and accessible sources of inspirational learning has been the game-changing work done by TED (Technology, Education and Design), a non-profit organisation dedicated to 'sharing ideas and sparking conversations that will change the world'. TED has brought innovators, inventors, scientists and pioneers to the notice of new audiences, who have amplified, shared or invested in new ideas. I passionately believe that hearing personal stories told in an authentic way sparks vital conversations that will galvanise action.

Inspired by this concept, I have hosted several events to bring great thinkers and storytellers to the attention of my own colleagues and clients. I am always on the lookout for outstanding people with great stories who can be a source of inspirational energy to others. Finding similar professional or innovative events in your sector, or even setting them up yourself, is a great way to bring fresh thinking into your organisation, and at little cost.

Among my favourite speakers on the topic of energy, and a great source of personal inspiration, is performance coach Paula Reid, who found fame in 2015 when she skied to the South Pole, one of the many bucket-list adventures she has identified for herself before she dies. Paula speaks passionately about how she prepared, what worked and what didn't, the horrible challenges she had faced and the sheer bliss of achieving an amazing feat.[12] Now when I think about going the extra mile and finding inner resource and energising others, I think of Paula, and her attitude inspires me.

AN ENERGETIC MINDSET: GET OUT OF YOUR COMFORT ZONE

When Paula is not sailing across the Atlantic or skiing to the South Pole, she is busy helping other people fulfil their goals. Here is her evidence:

> I prefer to adopt the 'step-up approach' to life as opposed to pursuing mindfulness and meditation. I am more of an activist, I like hands-on doing stuff and driving momentum. I've drawn up an amazing bucket list of all the places I want to see and things I want to do, and as fast as I cross some off, I keep adding some more.

Paula's philosophy is built on robust principles of positive psychology and a raw belief in individual capability and resilience. People have the choice between positive and negative beliefs, and when they choose to be positive they discover reserves of constructive energy and determination that enable them to move mountains.

> Standing still carries no rewards. We will learn less, be less capable and skilled, less wise and experienced. Taking the plunge on bold goals, whether mentally, physically, spiritually and emotionally, makes me feel more alive, motivated, focused and sharp. All the effort I make planning ahead and preparing for adventures is rewarded with a lifelong sense of achievement. Pain is temporary, pride is forever.

While sailing around the world or skiing to the South Pole may exceed most people's aspirations, taking part in a physical challenge that takes you outside of your comfort zone can be a highly inspirational experience. Many companies organise these as part of their corporate social responsibility programmes to engage employees in team activities that relate to their own purpose, offering them as incentives or rewards for high-performers. Others allow employees time off to undertake personal or charity challenges of their own, and support their fundraising efforts. Both options have been found to deliver enormous mutual benefits. People who take part in these challenges learn things about themselves, such as their physical and mental limits, and strategies to cope with new situations.

Emotional connection and inspiration

When people are energised by their work, or bring their positive emotional energy to the workplace, they not only achieve more for themselves but they also impact their friends, their families and their colleagues.

Organisations that create opportunities for people to achieve that level of engagement are the ones that will outlive and outperform their rivals. People who are open to be inspired go the extra mile, are happier, become leaders, and are most likely to provide inspiration to others.

I believe that employees and employers have a great deal of control over releasing the emotional energy that tilts the scale from complacent to committed, from having an average to an excellent experience at work.

Inspirational people and leadership

Adopting a positive outlook cannot be forced, but is a conscious, personal choice, and individuals can decide how much to give and take from the relationships around them. That goes for leaders, whose positions require them to positively influence others, as much as for any employee who can choose to be a proactive or reactive team player. But one acknowledged and decisive factor is the presence of an inspirational leader.

Inspiration is defined as the action or power that moves the intellect or changes the emotions. It is what makes you think or look at something differently. It can prompt a shift in spirit, in mood, in attitude. Inspiration creates positive energy.

Inspirational leaders tend to present a clear vision that is relevant and compelling. Academics Baker, Cross and Parker refer to the leadership quality of opening up the realms of realistic possibilities rather than zooming in on unattainable goals or targets.[13] But by far the most significant factor in inspiring teams is inclusivity, the ability to acknowledge and invite the contribution of other people, allowing for flexibility and shared responsibility in the delivery, rather than dictating too precisely how things should be done.

To inspire followers and supporters, leaders also need to be fully engaged in the moment of connection with others, demonstrating that they listen to and care about their teams. Inspirational leaders have been described as those who make their employees feel valued and special, and whose whole focus goes to the current conversation or agenda.

Employees must have confidence that a leader will deliver what he or she commits to, that they are trustworthy, and that they are committed to working together for results. Inspiration evokes a precious sense of shared focus and shared achievement, and that's what drives the sense of urgency and energy to get things done.

Beyond these core characteristics, inspirational leadership can appear in a number of guises, as evidenced by research issued by Bain in 2016 and listing thirty-three different leadership qualities that were regarded as inspirational.[14] Successful leaders offered several unique combinations of these, including a need for balance between exuding personal charisma and a heightened sensitivity to others. For example, being assertive and showing passion needed to be tempered by empathy and humility; personal vitality and authenticity should be supported by the ability to reach others and create inclusive conversations. To be inspired by their leaders, it appears that people needed to be able to relate to or connect with them on a personal level.

Tapping into collective energy

Leaders need followers, and followers with energy. In their book *Fully Charged*, business strategists Heike Bruch and Bernd Vogel explored the dynamics of collective energy and the contagious and infectious power of energy in organisations.[15] Rather than being the sole source of inspiration, leadership should engage others in understanding a shared goal, establish processes to encourage co-creation of strategies to achieve it, and spread the responsibility to their co-workers to be sources of vibrant energy. 'People become more in sync, share the same energy on a more intense level.' In practice, this shows itself in how excited employees are, how alert they are, and how much effort they put behind given strategies or in their own particular jobs.

How far your employees need to interact with each other is obviously driven by the work that your organisation does, but team dynamics make a crucial difference to the overall energy in a workplace. Shared goals bring people together on an intellectual as well as an emotional level, but the process of sharing thoughts and defining actions generally needs connection. Companies should provide opportunities for employees to share their ideas on core aspects of their business and make and own plans.

Companies like Siemens, Coca-Cola, Unilever and Mars promote a long heritage of discovery and invention, and this inspires other high achievers to join and make their own contribution to sustaining the value of these brands. They all have schemes that foster the generation of ideas, from internal cross-functional and cross-discipline think-tanks to open innovation events that bring inventors in from the outside world to share learning and thinking strategies. They each have their own culture, yet organisations that innovate on a grand scale, old or new, are built on networks of energy that generate ideas and then connect talent across traditional hierarchical boundaries.

Celebrating the energy inside

Pooling the expertise of employees has been proven to drive business assets such as innovation and problem-solving; and providing the forums for social interaction will yield the extra bonus of showing employees just how talented their own colleagues are.

One of the greatest attractions for candidates applying to high-performing organisations is the capability of the people they are likely to work with. Many organisations present their employees in their recruitment arena, as heroes who have invented something new, or persevered against all odds, or done something in an amazing way. Celebrating employees and their achievements inside the organisation is somehow rarer, and it is often a criticism from members in the companies I work with that there is very little exposure of how much 'good stuff' happens.

Organisations need to pay more attention to identifying and sharing the positive impacts of employees' work, and this can be done through simple storytelling channels in internal media and employee-recognition schemes. Employees' stories can also provide content for external media and other public accolades such as awards, which in turn have a huge impact on morale. True stories about real achievements are an important and often untapped source of inspiration to others.

Personal networks and support systems

Anyone who has been running a business in the last decade will know that the onslaught of disruptive competition so far this century has coincided with a worldwide recession, and economic recovery has been slow. It took five years, until the last quarter of 2013, for the UK economy to reach the levels of 2008, and a further two for GDP per head to return to pre-recession levels.[16] The result of the EU Referendum in 2016 and ongoing Brexit negotiations have made this a decade of uncertainty for consumers and businesses alike. Organisations that have survived have displayed various qualities, including leadership clarity and commitment, boldness, flexibility and a relentless attention to detail.[17] In my experience as a supplier to some of the world's largest companies and as an entrepreneur/employer during these tough times, professional inspiration and personal resilience have been at a premium.

Whether in or out of work during this period, running a business or part of a team, one of the most common concerns for the average person has been how to protect professional and personal living standards, how to deliver more for less, and how to maintain the energy to weather the financial storm. These are tough challenges and they aren't getting any easier. In the context of changing demographics and the fixed trend for longer working lives, there is an additional economic and physical imperative for all of us to learn how to recharge our emotional batteries.

Time and time again, I have found that having a support system in place, where one can draw on the experience and wisdom of other people, is hugely energising. I have sought this out proactively throughout my career by joining formal professional associations and by creating my own informal network of trusted peers, with whom I feel free to raise challenges and concerns.

For the last thirty years, along with my family at my core, I have felt energised by my relationships with clients and colleagues. I have sought inspiration from the outside world of art and literature, travel and culture, to do what I believe has been a great job, to lead a team and to come up with creative and relevant work.

In conclusion, my belief is that to survive in a competitive world, organisations need to put in place multiple policies and robust structures that protect the physical, mental and spiritual wellbeing and energy of their people. And at the same time, individuals need to nourish their own energy, to look after their physical health, to adopt a positive attitude, and make active and systematic efforts in quest of inspiration.

THE LONELINESS OF THE LONG-DISTANCE RUNNER

I once asked my good friend Steve Doswell, a communications consultant, and then CEO of the Institute of Internal Communication (IoIC), where he got his energy from. His answer was simple:

> As a self-employed communications professional? We need to find energy from each other. Communications people find themselves few in number and frequently alone in an organisation. While they may have learned the operational language of the organisation and of the specific sector in which it operates, it is a language second to their own.
>
> The communications person has to learn the skills of resilience and adaptability of those who live as foreigners outside their native land. That can be a lonely place, so they need to generate their own energy, be self-starters, find models, guides and mentors, read around their professional subject, take part in communication networking opportunities and find other ways to immerse themselves in their own profession, not least by becoming active in their own professional body.

In the case of the communicator, Steve referred to the IoIC and our peer practitioners within it as that professional community from which we could reliably draw strength. 'It's the oasis or the well that we know is always there even if our own workplace offers a more arid environment in terms of inspiration.'

This advice could cover people in other, specialised professions, or really anyone who finds themselves out on a limb in their working environment. It is a useful reminder of the positive emotional energy to be drawn from a personal network of people outside your immediate organisation but perhaps within your profession or sector.

Action Plan for Energy: How to create a positively energetic working environment that will sustain your organisation and its employees

Energy at work exposes the truly interdependent nature of the working relationship. Creating a safe and stimulating environment will feed your employees' energy. Their energy in turn will feed into your dynamic environment. The more you put in, the more you get out, and the greater the benefit for all, right? Right: but, if energy runs low in your organisation, brace yourself. To create a new dynamic at work doesn't come easy.

1. Energise yourself!
If you have decided to adopt the PRIDE model in your organisation, you will need to keep your own energy levels high. Positive energy is contagious, and as a voice for the PRIDE approach, you need to be a source of energy, an agent of change and an inspiration for other people. Think about your relationship with work, what prompts you to get up in the morning, what makes you feel most energised, and what gives you the greatest sense of fulfilment. Rehearse in your mind moments or days or events that made you feel good about yourself, your job, your team or your organisation. Your goal should be to feel those positive emotions more often, and to enable your colleagues to feel them too.

As you start to create an Energy Plan for your organisation, make sure that you continue to follow your own parallel plan that allows you to build your own physical fitness, keep a clear mind and find sources of positive emotion and inspiration that will give you the stamina and resilience to overcome setbacks.

2. Get help to scope your project
Remember that energy is a personal force to be reckoned with, and that, while your plan will include some aspects of organisational policy, it will be most effective if it taps into your employees' individual motivations. Gather a team of individuals

who can work with you to make sure that employee preferences have influence from the outset. And have a kick-off meeting. The Energy Plan comprises three main areas:

- the physical environment and employee health
- spurs for a lively and inquiring mind
- and sources of influence on personal connection and positivity.

Flesh out the meaning of these headings as they relate to your organisation, and identify the areas that you wish to address under each. Keep the energy high at that first meeting, with lots of water, fruit, energy drinks and chocolate bars. Think freely, tell stories, keep people moving around the room and encourage everyone to contribute. Keep your team energised by giving them clear tasks, freedom to express themselves, regular encouragement and feedback on progress and results.

3. The physical environment

Identify the aspects of your premises that impact physical energy. Does the layout of the office/factory/warehouse support your processes? Are people given the opportunity to interact with each other efficiently? Do employees enjoy enough light, heat and access to fresh air? Do you have the right combination of meeting rooms/ breakout rooms/open spaces/quiet working areas? Do people have any choice about where they sit for different tasks? Are you making the most of your premises to satisfy your organisational needs? For example, if your organisation relies on speed and agility, your employees need to move around easily and safely; if it relies on collaboration and new ideas, then you need to shape the physical space for people to work together and the setting for creative thought. Put yourself in your employees' shoes and think about whether your physical environment is fit for purpose.

4. Employee health: know the facts

Are your employees as healthy as they can be? Every organisation will be different, but you should investigate the trends on employee sickness, recurring conditions or other reasons for absence. Some offices, branches and shops are healthier than others. Find out what is going on at the healthy ones and create a best-practice checklist to support your plan. Investigate every opportunity you have in the workplace to influence good diet (e.g. by providing healthy options in canteens and vending machines) and exercise (e.g. by introducing options for physical activity in breaks during the working day).

Specific working conditions, such as shift work, night work, long-distance driving or constant international travel are proven to upset sleeping and eating patterns, and are likely to lead to greater alcohol and tobacco consumption. If your employees are required to work in any of these conditions, you should consider exploring preventative health measures: for example, special health education and awareness schemes to address the challenges.

5. Create thinking spaces at work

For a clear head or to create brain space, you have to give your employees the gift of time. Your Energy Plan should therefore provide ideas for managers and their teams on how to identify times and places in the working day that are free from continual activity, interruption and distraction. Think about these as breathing spaces for the mind, when employees can let go of their immediate concerns, allow their brains to relax and refresh their mental capacity. Thinking spaces can make room for individuals to practise mindfulness techniques, or groups to meet for problem-solving or creativity. If you need people to perform consistently under pressure, give them the means to recover; if you need new solutions, new ideas, give them conditions that conduce to creative thought. Woven around the demands of the organisation and the expectations you make of your employees, this part of the Energy Plan focuses on building positive mental energy and resilience.

6. Address negative energy

You also need to address the negative energy in your organisation, and its causes. Think about the times when you have felt that your organisation was under pressure. It could be related to periods of peak demand, increasing workload, particular points in your production cycle, poor management, or a department that is going through organisational change such as relocation or restructuring. Your Energy Plan should contain features that will alleviate some of the stress points; for example, by providing coaching to leaders dealing with new situations, or positive backing and recognition to people enduring exceptional or uncertain times. Showing that you understand the difficulties in an organisation will give your employees more confidence in your judgement. It may also alleviate the pressure on them, as they will feel less isolated in their challenge.

7. Find out what makes people feel good and how to make that the norm

The last part of your Energy Plan will address softer subjects like behaviours, values, feelings and emotions. It requires you to sketch the working environment that will meet both your organisational purpose and your employees' motivations. You will have to cover aspects that represent your organisation as it is, to detail how you wish it to become, but also to identify conditions that connect individuals to each other and to a collective goal.

How would you describe the type of organisation you are currently in? What is it like to work there? Is this the kind of workplace that you and your colleagues want to be part of? Go back to the questions you asked yourself in section 1 and project them onto your colleagues. Are your employees currently energised? When and how? And how can you make them feel more energised, more often? Draw up a list of factors that deliver the most positive experiences.

In my experience, these will include times when they have enjoyed working with other like-minded, talented people, or they have made an emotional or social connection with co-workers. They may have worked on a new product design, learned something new or been involved in an exciting project. They have been stretched, coached to success and recognised for their efforts. They have worked for an inspirational leader, or they themselves have led a team through a challenge. Or they may simply have had fun, or laughed out loud at work.

Discover what makes your employees feel motivated, energised, inspired, and then find the means to deliver those conditions. For many of us, an energetic workplace is one where people have close relationships and mutual respect, where experiences and emotions are shared and celebrated. Where managers and leaders understand how to enthuse themselves and those around them. Where people enjoy the freedom to learn, grow and seek inspiration from each other and from the outside.

Your Energy Plan will help you discover what creates positive energy in your organisation, and then find ways to feed and nurture it. Adopt these principles and make them your own. Tapping into the sources of positive energy and inspiration will make your workplace an emotionally healthy and stimulating environment that will survive.

8. Bringing it all together

Remember that the three areas of organisational and personal energy that we have discussed interact and impact on each other. It is hard to imagine an emotionally animated workplace where the physical conditions are appalling; or an inspirational environment where individuals are constantly exhausted. It is possible for people to put in extraordinary efforts for a compelling purpose, to pay no heed to their physical health, and to survive on adrenalin for a while. But these conditions are not sustainable. A look at the longest-surviving organisations – and the best of the new corporate giants who are creating the conditions for a longer life – reveals a holistic approach. Their success is built on a sustained effort to deal with each aspect of organisational and personal energy – whether physical, mental or emotional.

How does Energy fit into the PRIDE model?

Within the PRIDE model, Energy is the fuel that drives people to engage in all aspects of their work, to take a challenge, carry out a task, fulfil a purpose, live up to a reputation. It sets free the physical and emotional effort that makes people perform at their best and reap the rewards.

Energy is personal and it is collective. It will feed and be fed by individual motivation, participation, ability and resilience. Personally, it can be innate, it can be created, it can be nourished and it can be drained. Positive energy can spark innovation; negative energy can kill an idea. Collectively, energy can be channelled to deliver an organisation's promise to its customers and its employees, brilliantly and with pride.

At the same time, energy is a product of the other factors of the PRIDE model. It will thrive in an organisation where people are inspired by its purpose and feel that their efforts yield some greater good, where they are convinced of the value and integrity of its reputation, and where they believe and are invested in its future direction. Energy, along with purpose, reputation, integrity and direction, is welded to personal and organisational performance. These are the factors that culminate in pride.

6
PRIDE in Practice

I hope I have inspired you to think differently about engaging people behind organisational goals and have convinced you of the power of Purpose, Reputation, Integrity, Direction and Energy in building success for your organisation and your employees.

Through the Action Plans in each chapter, I have shown how the PRIDE principles can spur on practical activities in any workplace situation and better the working experience for thousands of people.

In this final chapter I shall cover the remaining questions of where to start with launching a programme and how to judge its impact. I shall introduce the PRIDE Diagnostic, which will serve you to benchmark your current levels of employee pride and identify key areas to address. I will also suggest ways to establish a team of PRIDE Practitioners to champion and communicate the programme. And I shall touch on the concept of Moments of PRIDE, an idea to highlight and celebrate positive results that can be shared across your organisation and bring momentum for ongoing activity.

Every reader, every leader or potential influencer who embarks on the PRIDE model will be meeting with different combinations of organisational strengths and weaknesses. Every organisation stands on a different starting line and so will need a bespoke programme and activation team to implement the PRIDE model. Depending on the size of your organisation and the level of expertise of your team, you may need to bring in outside support.* Yet my aim in this chapter is to provide a common methodology

---

* Advice on external support for a PRIDE programme can be found on www.takepride.co.

that will show readers how to create a PRIDE programme for their own organisations.

How to build PRIDE

Creating the diagnostic

The Centre for Brand Analysis (TCBA) provides research, data analysis and consultancy to a wide range of business-to-consumer and business-to-business brands across a variety of sectors. TCBA also produces a portfolio of annual brand barometers, including Superbrands and CoolBrands, which have been recognised as key indices of UK brand performance for twenty-four and seventeen years respectively. I chose TCBA to review the PRIDE model from the perspective of external branding and the customer experience. Founder and CEO Stephen Cheliotis first validated the importance of the five component parts of the PRIDE model, in terms of their impact on employee experience and perception of the brand (see above). We then worked together to create a diagnostic tool that measures the levels of employee pride in the organisation.

Validation of the five components of PRIDE by Stephen Cheliotis

In external brand engagement, people make decisions about the brands they consume and buy into based on a combination of rational and emotional factors, including learned experience, considered evaluation, emotional impressions and spontaneous thought. Brands live in consumers' minds or hearts. There isn't a single definitive description of what a brand is, but I adhere to this one by American author Marty Neumeier: 'A brand is a person's gut feeling about a product, service or organisation.' Faced with a purchasing decision, consumers will typically decide whether to buy one brand over another in seconds, depending on this predisposition, as well as on its availability and dominance in the market.

Similarly, in the employment arena, potential employees will decide whether to engage with an organisation, based on their experience and impression of that brand, and make a fairly spontaneous decision about a brand's suitability for them, even making a sweeping assessment on whether they love or hate that brand. Of course, existing employees have a great deal more rational experience of what it is like to work for a particular brand, but there are still several emotional layers at play in their overall evaluation of the organisation, and engagement with their role within it.

Purpose: The purpose of a company is a core driver of commercial performance and stakeholder engagement.[1] Successful consumer brands understand that emotional connection delivers customer loyalty and engagement, and consumers are increasingly demanding of brands to demonstrate who they are and what they stand for. Similarly, brands are being expected to articulate what they stand for to their internal stakeholders. The message in the recruitment arena is 'This is what we believe in and what we are trying to achieve, and if you believe in these as well, join us.' The motivation works for employee retention, too, for if people believe in the purpose of the brand they are more likely not only to want to join a company but also to stick around as well.

Reputation: The idea of working for a renowned brand has an important impact on employee motivation. All the metrics show that those working for well-regarded brands are more likely than employees of lesser-known brands to recommend their companies' products (by an uplift of 30 per cent).[2] In consumer branding, winning market share depends on being front of mind; similarly, to build an employer brand, you need to occupy the entry points for people looking for employment.

Integrity: Delivering your brand promise is a fundamental rule of marketing, and it has to happen at every touch point, with excellent products, service and customer relations. Similarly, in your relationship with employees, if you don't deliver, people won't give you the benefit of the doubt more than once or twice. Increasingly, brands are being asked about ethical aspects of their business too, from product sourcing to employment conditions. You can't hide any more. People will find out if you are not living up to your promises and responsibilities. Whether you fail to deliver for your customers, or you fail to deliver for your employees, people will eventually leave you.

Direction: Successful organisations provide people with the information they need to determine where they are heading and what their role is within the big picture. Employers who set out clear direction and enable their employees to perform and develop constantly outperform their rivals. Just by being the most visible, the brand leader in each category has a huge advantage in terms of public acceptance, whether that is by the media, customers or employees. But resting on your laurels is not an option, and there have been many victims of change and disruptive innovation that have fallen off the consumer and, subsequently, the employment radar. In order to survive, organisations need to evolve, and they need to bring their employees with them on that journey.

Energy: It is no accident that some of the brand leaders in the FMCG market of 1916 were still brand leaders in 2016. They work tirelessly to attract the best people, build the best reputation and sustain positive energy to drive longevity. In the UK, British Airways sustained its place as the most successful brand for decades. Yet in 2012 BA recognised that in spite of being a good brand and having a lot of goodwill, it needed to refresh and re-energise itself so as to prove to its stakeholders that it could still innovate and do interesting things. The London Olympic sponsorship was a massive opportunity to reinvigorate the brand externally and internally, and the company ran an integrated communications campaign that reflected the spirit of the brand across all stakeholder groups. British Airways reaped the benefit in terms of employee engagement, customer experience, customer spend and stakeholder advocacy.

Collectively, these elements of the brand identity impact on me, on my decisions as a human being, and a consumer, on what is suitable for me, and what is not, and on how I engage with the organisation. I am convinced that the elements of the PRIDE model are five proven factors that contribute to overall employee engagement as well.

The diagnostic tool – understanding your starting point

The PRIDE model aims to create a strong intellectual and emotional connection between an employer and its employees, and so the first step is to measure the reach and positivity of the present relationship. The diagnostic contains a qualitative assessment and a quantitative employee questionnaire, testing how all five elements of the PRIDE model are working in your organisation.

The research process starts with individual, in-depth, structured interviews with an organisation's leadership team that examine their perception of the current state of pride in the organisation. Ideally, an independent researcher should conduct this self-assessment and then put it to the test internally with representative employee focus groups and personal observations. The idea is to draw up a common perspective on the workplace through the collective opinions of key stakeholders, whether these show a shared opinion or divergent views.

The quantitative questionnaire then tests the broad reality of the employees' experience with a representative sample of employees. The number of participants depends on the size and complexity of the organisation, and should entail multiple locations, functions, job roles and employee demographics. The questionnaire can be conducted online or by hard copy, depending on the working practices of the organisation.

The full questionnaire requires up to 100 individual responses to questions and statements in twelve different categories. The questions and statements are variously related to different aspects of the PRIDE model, and are spread across multiple categories. Respondents are not immediately aware of the way their responses connect to the five factors of PRIDE. The number of questions and statements can be tailored to fit the target user group, but there is a minimum set of questions that are required before an integrated PRIDE score can be arrived at. Organisations wishing to test other aspects of employee opinion and emotions may add specific additional questions of their own.

Typically, the questionnaire will contain the following core questions

Purpose: How well is the purpose understood in the organisation? Did the purpose attract you to the company in the first place? Is there evidence of it in practice? Are employees measured and rewarded by behaviour that helps achieve the purpose?

Reputation: Are you perceived to have built an excellent reputation? Are you considered a leader in your category? Do your organisation's leaders stand out? Can your brand survive a crisis?

Integrity: How far is the brand delivered internally, and do employees perceive that it delivers for customers too? Are you listening to customer feedback, and acting on it? Do employees feel they are given the tools and resources needed to do their job? Is yours an enjoyable place to work?

Direction: Is your leadership team positive and effective? What are the long-term prospects for your organisation? How far are employee motivations understood at work? How far do employees understand the big picture, and are they empowered to deliver it?

Energy: How far does the organisation protect itself against risks? How well does it manage its employee wellbeing? Do employees have the opportunity to engage in activities outside of work? Does the organisation promote positive workplace energy?

Analysing the response

Questionnaire responses are first analysed by category of question, and a score for the entire organisation is assigned to each component part of the PRIDE model. A single score for the global organisational pride is arrived at by combining the five factors.

Additional fields of research can be placed in the questionnaire to enable deeper analysis of the data. For example, responses can be segmented by location, function or job levels, to reflect the operational structure of the organisation.

Distributed through the questionnaire are a number of so-called 'killer questions', such as asking respondents to rate their current levels of pride and how far they would recommend their employers to others. These questions centre on metrics that are deemed vital indicators of internal brand equity.

The PRIDE diagnostic will demonstrate where the strengths and weaknesses of the organisation lie and enable you to pinpoint the areas most in need of attention. For organisations that are new to the concept of employee engagement, there may be some fresh practices to put in place and some minimum standards to set, across all aspects of the PRIDE model. For others, there may be one or more clear areas of improvement to be made to counterbalance inconsistencies between scores.

It is also possible to discover some interdependencies and correlations, where a single factor counteracts more than one PRIDE component. In this case, you may find that one course of corrective action addresses more than one weakness. The results for each organisation will be unique, and the improvement programme will need to be tailored accordingly.

Action Plans

You will find ideas for improvement on all aspects of the PRIDE model in the Action Plan sections at the end of the five opening chapters. There are also several insights from individual leaders and influencers who have put some of these ideas into action and achieved high scores in these areas.

The time frame for your programme will depend on the scale of your organisation and the requirements identified in the first diagnostic. However, your team will need at least six to twelve months to put its first improvement plans into practice.

Tracking progress

There are several ways of conducting light-touch reviews of your action plans, including informal feedback sessions with employee representatives, and quick pulse surveys on one or two aspects of your programme. In order to track results of the entire programme, you need to repeat the entire diagnostic twelve to eighteen months after the first one.

Increased levels of pride may lie a few steps away, or they may require a lengthy iterative process. But having seen and felt the positive impact of simple actions time and time again, given the right leadership, task force and attitude, increased levels of pride at work are a completely achievable ambition.

Establishing PRIDE Practitioners

To establish and conduct a PRIDE programme calls for leadership, ownership and resource. When it comes to people policies and change, few organisations start with a blank sheet of paper: there will be history and culture, strategic priorities and policies, legacy systems and processes, personalities and egos for you to manage.

In smaller companies, a single, strong influencer could set the PRIDE programme rolling. To fully realise the programme in larger organisations, the process will involve convincing others to sponsor it, building a team, or summoning outside expertise. Right from the start, you will have to manage the expectations of your leadership team and see that they are aligned with the goals of the programme.

The resourcing and structure of the action team will depend on where you sit in your organisation. If you are the CEO, appoint a programme manager to be your right hand and coordinator. If you are not the CEO, then get his or her immediate backing. Ideally, the sponsor should be one of your board members – if not the CEO, then a director of HR, communications, brand – but no matter what their title, they should have a mandate for people and/or brand and be well networked across the organisation.

Organisations large and small adopt process-improvement and employee-engagement programmes with and without outside assistance. However, few programmes succeed without a team of professional enthusiasts to champion the cause. Gather as many of your team as you can from the inside, and share with them the principles of the PRIDE philosophy. Giving them the title of PRIDE Practitioners will give them, and your programme, a cohesive identity within your organisation.

This team needs to represent the power base and structure of the organisation. By *power base*, I mean the people who make the decisions and who drive the business. By *structure* I mean where employees are based, what the functions and hierarchies are and how they operate. You should involve employee representatives from any existing union arrangements, with the guidance of your HR/ Employee Relations lead.

Communicating PRIDE

The PRIDE model is designed to work around existing organisational practices and communications channels, and does not assume the need for big communications campaigns. However, you will have to take a strategic and coordinated approach to spelling out exactly how the research and analysis phase will work, and be ready to issue results and improvement plans afterwards. The more transparent you are about the whole programme, the more likely that all your employees will understand, be receptive and get on board.

Embarking on employee research raises expectations, and you or your chosen team need to be genuinely committed to the principles of making improvements, before defining what these need to be. You also need to keep line managers informed and involved in the objectives of the programme, and on board with its implications. The programme is likely to call for some elements of process or behavioural change that other staff will need to carry out, so these should be passed on with clarity and supported where necessary by skills development and coaching.

Celebrating Moments of PRIDE

The final part of the PRIDE implementation and communications plan will be a process to recognise and celebrate good results. If you already have an employee-recognition scheme, you should consider whether to integrate elements of the PRIDE programme into it, or to expand it to include improvements seen as a result.

Recognition is a vital source of motivation for employees. Stories of successful people and events create energy that is positively contagious. If you have no scheme in place, you are missing a widely accepted way to motivate and engage your teams. Adopt a simple approach that is based on the elements of the PRIDE model and their impacts on people and the business. Define Moments of PRIDE in terms that suit your organisation, describe the types of experiences you want your employees to share, then provide the means to do that in a physical space or through one of your current communications channels.

Create a process that will suit the culture of your organisation and consider how to encourage people to take part. Giving employees the freedom to express themselves will add to the authenticity of the PRIDE programme and share ownership of the scheme.

My moments of pride

I began this book with a story of a time when I felt disenchanted with work, when I had a rotten boss, hated going to work and had no confidence in what I had to do when I got there. I was intrigued by what the company did, but rarely saw the outputs and felt no pride in my role. The only good I took from the experience was the decision I made never to work in such conditions again. I would spend as much of my working life as possible doing what I loved, doing it well and doing it for people who cared.

To round off my story, I would like to share better memories of two great occasions when I achieved that goal. These are two of my own special moments of pride. Strangely, they took place in the same company around the same time, but they demonstrate two entirely different aspects of what pride can feel like – one very personal, the other on a corporate scale.

It was the year 2003 or 2004 at theblueballroom and I was working on a contract to produce a management magazine for DHL, called *The Network*. One day the phone rang in the office and I learned that one of the DHL directors was on the line. My heart almost stopped. My stomach fell into my boots. My first thought was what had I done wrong. I took the phone. 'I have called to say thank you,' the gravelly voice announced. My stomach bounced back into place. 'I'm at head office', he said, 'and have just been stopped in the corridor by a new member of the team, and he told me that he had just read the interview I gave in *The Network*. He said he read it and that it had confirmed all the reasons why he wanted to work for this company!'

'That's really wonderful. Thanks for telling me that', I said.

'I know that you wrote that report', said the director. 'So I just thought you should know that it landed really well. Thanks again for the really great work!'

The call must have taken about two minutes in all. It happened more than ten years ago, but I remember it in vivid detail. The fact that someone so busy and so senior, a client far removed from our work environment, had taken the time to call their supplier was a very big deal. That one short call told me that my work had been good and that it had made an impact; but what mattered most to me was that I felt valued. And that made me feel proud.

I can be more precise about the timing of the second moment, as it followed hours after the news of the colossal earthquake under the Indian Ocean that struck on Boxing Day 2004 and set off a tsunami that caused devastation across much of South East Asia, claiming over 200,000 lives. I was at home with my husband and children, and we were enjoying a happy family Christmas. We watched the TV news with sudden horror, and felt we just wanted to 'do something' – but what?

That night I had a call from one of my clients at DHL, wanting to discuss how the story was breaking and what would need to be reported inside the company over the coming days, when I returned to work.[3] DHL had worked in the aftermath of natural disasters before, and was a founder member of the World Economic Forum's Disaster Relief Network (DRN). This network provided immediate help in disaster zones, with DHL offering logistics resource and know-how to deliver relief and humanitarian aid to places that had had their normal lines of communications and transportation broken.

My client told me that night that our mutual friend and close colleague Chris Weeks, DHL's Disaster Recovery Network Director, had already left his home near Brussels, bound for Asia. It turned out that Chris would lead a logistics team headquartered in Colombo, Sri Lanka, and would spend the next few months working day and night to get urgently needed aid and supplies to inaccessible areas in the tsunami-hit region. At that moment, from the comfort of my own home, I felt humbled. Humbled in the knowledge that someone I knew well was going to be part of this vast effort. Humbled that he, a parent like me, was going to step out of his family celebrations and go and do something quite exceptional on the other side of the world for other people. At the same time, I felt proud. Proud of him, of course, but also proud of the corporation that enabled this to happen. Unlike the earlier moment of pride, which had been personal, this felt far more substantial, more collective. This time, it was recognition of the power and goodwill of the brand that I was associated with. I have recalled this moment several times since Boxing Day 2004; it has always served to reinforce for me the positive, principled and ultimately responsible nature of DHL's ethos and values.

These two moments point to distinctly different aspects of pride that I have felt about work. The first stemmed from receiving recognition of the quality and perceived value of my own efforts, something I had done, and reaped the credit for. It met my motivational needs for making an impact and gaining professional respect from the highest level. At the time in my career when I was setting up a creative services agency, this gave me credibility in front of my team and other clients. The second experience had much more to do with feeling moved by someone else's actions, and taking pride in being associated with a company and a brand that was doing something good and important. At that point, I respected DHL because, as a corporation, it had not only made a commitment to doing something vital in the wake of a disaster, but had founded a culture that inspired and enabled dedicated individuals to take leave of their homes at Christmas to make it happen.

I have been fortunate enough to have many moments of pride in my working life, and I relish every one of them. I have also tried to create similar moments for other people who work with me, whether they are clients or colleagues. I hope this book will inspire and enable you to take the PRIDE model to the heart of your organisation, because I simply believe that pride at work makes for a better life.

Take PRIDE in the future

When in 2014 the FTSE 100 celebrated its thirtieth anniversary,[4] only thirty of the original hundred listed great British companies appeared in the index, and only nineteen of those (names like Barclays, BP, Marks & Spencer, Unilever) had never dropped out of it. Corporations that had once seemed fireproof had shrunk, been broken up, sold or disappeared without trace, and been replaced by new names from the UK's buoyant digital and mobile technology sector, as well as by an increased number of foreign companies listed in London. Sectors that had suffered included traditional consumer products, travel companies and retail chains, which had been slow to react to new technology, customer demands or competition.

The corporate landscape remains volatile, and in 2016 the average life expectancy even of the largest global corporations was twenty-four years, and falling every year.[5] At the same time, the outlook for start-ups is bleak: almost half of UK SMEs founded in the last decade have failed to celebrate their fifth birthday. The reasons cited in the UK are cash-flow issues, lack of bank lending, competition and generally poor follow-through to scale up to demand.

So how do great companies, large and small, survive and thrive, and move confidently with the times? According to most commentators, they stay close to their customers, are open to learn new technologies, channels and business models, and reinvest their profits in product and service enhancements. But they also attract talented people, retain their entrepreneurial spirit, remain open-minded and agile, and harness innovation. Many of the giants – Unilever, P&G, Mars, Coca-Cola – have held on to their founders' core purpose, but they have refreshed them and made them relevant to new generations of consumers and employees. Rather than rest on their laurels, they seek constant innovation to fortify sustainability.

In spite of the odds, entrepreneurial spirit remains strong in the UK, with the number of start-ups growing year on year. According to recent studies, new companies take off because of good ideas occurring at the right time,[6] but they take hold on the market when they master the ability to scale, including being able to recruit and motivate others who can deliver on their core proposition.

Large or small, your organisation's lasting success depends on your employees' performance, and this springs entirely from the conditions you create for them at work. The PRIDE model is one way to deliver the very best conditions that will create and nurture deep and lasting relationships between your organisation and your people.

I have drawn the core elements of the PRIDE model from thirty years of professional experience, working with the employers of tens of thousands of people in some of the world's market-leading and most complex organisations, as well as employing my own staff for more than fifteen years. They have emerged from hours and days of listening and observing people at work at all levels, as I tried to make sense of what makes them tick as individuals and as teams, and to do the right thing by them.

I have applied all my intuition and imagination to create something important and memorable, and to articulate it in a way that has meaning and relevance to others. I regard PRIDE as a universal model of building organisational and personal success in the workplace. Universal for organisations, because it carries robust evidence about how organisations develop and function. Universal for people, because it draws on certain truths about what people look for at work.

This book is its first full articulation.

I am now embarking on the next stage of my professional adventure, and hoping to share the PRIDE model with a wider world. I want its impact to reach beyond my own consultancy and beyond my clients into other, broader, fields. I want to reach leaders and influencers wherever they are, in the private, the public or the third sector, in the UK and around the world. I want to reach the employers of people everywhere, who seek and deserve to feel pride in who they are and what they do. I want them to take pride to work and for work to be better.

The last word: a leader's perspective

In a world of constant business transformation, it feels, that many leaders tend to lose sight of the vital few things to ultimately shift gears in their organisations. Those things are customer-centricity and employee-centricity: Creating customer excitement goes hand in hand with your employees feeling 'this is a great place to work'. The more experience I gain, the more I recognise that what one might expect to be very commonplace is, in fact, rare, precious and yet crucial to success.

– Friedrich Georg-Lischkee

Friedrich Georg-Lischke was appointed CEO of Mars Drinks Europe just as the economic crisis of 2008–9 broke. He managed the business through a period of market contraction, where he was tasked with rebuilding both financial and in-market performance as well as employee pride in the brand. He was successful on all counts through a strategy of transformation that, for him, meant driving a culture of organisational excellence and individual contribution as much as changing the game behind strategy evolution and business innovation.

Working with Friedrich during his time at Mars Drinks gave me fresh insight into a leader's perspective on business and people, and due to a shared passion for both, the experience was pivotal in the development of the PRIDE model. For Friedrich, communication was like a religion, and he had utter faith in its value. I saw him listen, think, negotiate and convince, to unite and involve people around a shared purpose, to help them understand a change in business direction, and even to accept tough decisions. For him, authentic leadership met a fundamental human need: to be in good hands, to feel safe, to trust. Trust can sometimes be earned by doing what you say you will do. But, for Friedrich, 'just doing' was simply not good enough. He always did it with passion and pride. Here he shares his thoughts on building employee pride and why he believes that successful leadership will always have to be based on compatible personal and organisational values.

SP: How would you describe your leadership style?

FG-L: Great question! It certainly has evolved over the years – through feedback, self-reflection and observing great and not-so-great role models. What has been constant throughout my career is my belief in people and that everyone principally wants to grow and do better. Freedom is extremely important to me – so I want to pass it on to others. However, this comes along with my expectation of mutuality that is guarded by some degree of contract or framework. People who know me describe me as a present, approachable leader. I strive for clarity of shared targets and roles and am accountable for whole team performance.

SP: How do you approach a new challenge, or a new role?

FG-L: My approach has four key strands: customer, focus, people and agility.

You have to start out with your **customer** first and identify what is the value you provide to them to justify their attention. I engage the whole cross-functional team in defining the USP and identifying what it takes to drive that uniqueness across the organisation. The **customer** voice needs to be heard in every part of your organisation, in your decision-making processes, at your team meetings and in your market reviews. What your customers say about you defines your reputation. I encourage people to spend time with their customers, to know what they are thinking and to act on their opinions.

Whatever the sector, we need **focus** to break through complexity. In my experience, I have been constantly faced by endless possibilities but limited resources. Leaders can be overtaken by their ambition, by the scale of their opportunity and the variety of their options. **Focus** is about making a complex world less complicated, deciding on your solution, allocating your resources according to priority, and delivering higher quality as a result. It's the same for communications: focus brings clarity, so much so that leaders are sometimes surprised by how simply something can be communicated. I recommend everyone to look at their strategy, and if you cannot express it in simple words to someone who has no clue about your business, think again.

The success of any strategy depends on having enough of the right **people** to own and implement it. Individuals of appropriate talent, experience and potential, equipped with a positive attitude. And that is where the PRIDE model comes in. I would like to highlight the crucial importance of gaining the confidence of the people that work for you. They actually spend the majority of their lives at work! Aspiring to engage with them feels like common sense; however, it is much easier said than done. To me, leadership is not a reward or a privilege – it's a responsibility. If you want people to follow a direction and take pride in their work, you need to first earn their trust. You will need to show you are present, you care and you are genuinely motivated to add value to them and to society, as well as to the business.

I strongly believe that **people** need to have the right rational rewards for their jobs, the right pay and so on, but they also need to know that they can do something good at work. If you can make them part of a common purpose, you have the foundation of an effective team. Great leadership is also about valuing the contribution of individuals and encouraging people to start taking joint responsibility and accountability. It can be a fairly typical instinct for someone in a leadership role, especially in a difficult situation, to take control, but as soon as you do so, you are working as one person and not as a stronger team.

Last but not least, to survive, progress, or adapt to market forces, organisations need **agility**. We as leaders have to ensure the right roles, processes and behaviours exist to make great ideas ultimately happen. I have seen so many good strategies or plans fail or businesses stagnate, when leaders got stuck on the strategic level and were not interested in the details of how it was going to happen. A winning concept is not enough, you also need to bring it to market. You need to have stamina and I like to create a sense of energy and commitment to turning strategy into action.

SP: Let's talk a little more now about how communications impacts engagement with your people.

FG-L: My deep conviction is that people engagement and customer engagement go hand in hand and they are hugely connected. We all know that a customer calling in to a company, whether it is a call centre or shop or head office, can clearly distinguish between an engaged or disengaged member of staff. Positive people engagement delivers a much better customer experience, and we all aspire to achieving that. In my experience, the process of changing a company from a negative or disengaged state to a more collaborative customer-centric culture, and of releasing those new more positive behaviours, has been a highly unifying experience for employees.

Everything around engagement with people requires you to tap into the rational and the emotional. And communication plays a pivotal role here. Yes, you need a meaningful business strategy, people need to understand where they are headed and have some evidence of why it will work. But you also need emotional intelligence. Leaders have to understand that not all people are the same. For some, change is an opportunity, for others it is a risk. And as a leader, you have to be close to your people, and know how they feel about things, as well as what they know.

You have crystallised these principles in the PRIDE model, and, as you point out, understanding who your people are, what they care about, what stage they are in their lives and their careers is hugely important. People need to satisfy their professional ambitions, but they also have home lives and they need a solution to both. If a company can provide an answer to that burning question, it really will achieve employee engagement. I have seen examples of people who are parents, or those with older dependants, working shifts to fit in with their care arrangements, and being totally committed to their job, and yet so many companies remain inflexible and insensitive to employees' needs. To get employees to engage with you, you have to be present, listen, listen, listen, and communicate, communicate, communicate! Engage with them as people first, and mean it.

SP: Do you really try to engage all employees?

FG-L: When it comes to engaging a team, there are always people who are ready to make a commitment, people who are already positively disposed to an organisation and its direction. These people may be leaders at different levels in the organisation and will gather support, but they are also ready to follow, to be part of something bigger.

The first challenge comes from people who are somehow in the middle, as you would say, 'on the fence'. My approach is to invite these team members to have a conversation about what really has to happen for them to be engaged. And then to try to show them how they could become more involved, more fulfilled. But I acknowledge also that engagement is not only the leader's responsibility. Every individual has a choice and is primarily accountable for his or her own personal fulfilment. Actually, that's where a lot of leaders get it wrong; passive participation is not the same as engagement. To make a difference, you need active contributors.

And the second obvious challenge for leaders will be the team members who are actively disengaged. As much as you have to demonstrate the types of behaviour you want to create, to lead by example, to reward and incentivise others to follow, you also have to identify what is not acceptable and, in my experience, take out those who are not willing to change. Leaders need to deal with conflict, negotiation and failure in order to show there are consequences of disengagement and to limit the impact of those that are 'poisoning the well'.

I have been influenced by and really benefited from an almost institutionalised all-employee engagement approach at Mars. I have seen it work, big time. And there is no half-baked approach to it. So, I would say to those leaders who are still hesitating about engaging with their employees: be aware, you won't attract the next generation or build a sustainable company, if you do not!

SP: How far is your leadership style grounded in your personal values?

FG-L: I think my leadership style is entirely driven by my personal values, and I would hope that other people might arrive at a similar point. It is self-evident that people are more collaborative and productive when their own beliefs match the values and culture of their co-workers. I do not believe that people can have two value sets – one in business life, another in private. In my mind, you cannot authentically sustain your values in a kind of role-play. My personal values, for instance, centre on achievement, excitement and mutuality, they are filters through which I can explain all I have done and feel, what has or has not worked. They have a massive impact on my approach and what I choose to do in life. They are the first thing I tell people about me when introducing myself to them as a leader and colleague.

Achievement for me is more than a personal best. I am excited about overcoming challenges. I am more fascinated by grasping opportunities than avoiding risks. Similarly, I try to break through structures or systems that hold me back. I enjoy benefiting from the diversity of teams and developing them to their next level. I get frustrated if people don't share my passion.

Mutuality is a core principle of Mars and is about gaining experience from the generosity of others and giving something back. It is about fairness, responsibility and respect. A promise is a promise. I have also been open to coaching, to self-reflection and to criticism from peers and subordinates. In order to win respect, you need to be able to acknowledge your weaknesses. Mutuality is a term I use now, having worked in Mars, but I think it was always there as a principle for me and in the way I was brought up.

What I see and appreciate about the PRIDE Model is the mutuality of respect between the organisation and individual – in my terms, being customer-centric and employee-centric in equal measure. If we expect people to bring their whole selves to work, and to engage in the goals of an organisation, then we must, as leaders, also engage with them. The principle of considering both these perspectives is highly authentic and to be recommended for today's and tomorrow's leaders.

Notes

Chapter 1: Purpose

[1] www.jimstengel.com/grow/research-validation/

[2] www.hbr.org/resources/pdfs/comm/ey/19392HBRReportEY.pdf. Harvard Business School Publishing (2015), 'The Business Case for Purpose'

[3] www.businesscommission.org

[4] www.theguardian.com/society/2015/apr/19/britain-uncovered-survey-attitudes-beliefs-britons-2015

[5] Lynda Gratton (2011), *The Shift*, Collins

[6] Women in Business Institute, London Business School (2009), *The Reflexive Generation: Young Professionals' Perspectives on Work, Career and Gender*

[7] www2.deloitte.com/global/en/pages/about-deloitte/articles/gx-millennials-shifting-business-purpose.html#, and www.pwc.com/gx/en/services/people-organisation/publications/workforce-of-the-future.html

[8] John Elkington and Pamela Hartigan (2008), *The Power of Unreasonable People: How Social Entrepreneurs Create Markets That Change the World*, Harvard Business School Publishing

[9] www.huffingtonpost.com/adam-grant/millennial-generation-jobs_b_3696622.html

[10] www.julianbirkinshaw.com/reinventing-management/

[11] Will McInnes (2012), *Culture Shock*, Wiley

[12] Jim Stengel (2012), *Grow*, Random House

[13] Jim Collins (2001), *Good to Great*, HarperCollins

[14] Jim Collins and Jerry Porras (1994), *Built to Last*, HarperCollins

15 www.marketingmagazine.co.uk/article/1383325/brand-purpose-isnt-just-layer-selling-products-says-p-gs-roisin-donnelly

16 www.marketingmagazine.co.uk/article/1344079/unilevers-keith-weed-brands-purpose-deliver-growth

17 www.ey.com/GL/en/Issues/Business-environment/ey-world-economic-forum-2015 www.ey.com/Publication/vwLUAssets/ey-the-business-case-for-purpose/$FILE/ey-the-business-case-for-purpose.pdf

18 www.theatlantic.com/health/archive/2011/08/maslow-20-a-new-and-improved-recipe-for-happiness/243486/

19 www.simplypsychology.org/maslow.html

20 Abraham H. Maslow (1997), *Motivation and Personality*, Harper & Row, first published in 1954

21 www.betterworkingworld.ey.com/#home

22 Simon Sinek (2009), *Start with Why*, Portfolio

Chapter 2: Reputation

1 The 2018 UK Reputation Dividend Report

2 The Reputation Institute, 'Annual Reptrak®Research 2014–2017'

3 www.pwc.com/gx/en/hr-management-services/publications/assets/ceosurvey-talent-challenge.pdf.

4 The top twenty names were taken from 2017 listings of: Interbrand's Best Global Brands, Brand Finance Most Valuable Brands, Times Top 100 Graduate Opportunities, Universum's Most Attractive Employers (among Engineering/IT/Business Students) and LinkedIn's World's 100 Most InDemand Employers

5 *The Cluetrain Manifesto* by Rick Levine, Christopher Locke, Doc Searls and David Weinberger first appeared on the web in 1999 and was published by Basic Books in 2000

6 Employer Branding International, '2014 Employer Branding Global Trends Study Report'

Chapter 3: Integrity

1 Institute of Directors in association with Cass Business School (2015), *The Great Governance Debate – Towards a Good*

Governance Index for Listed Companies

2 Simon Barrow and Richard Mosley (2005), *The Employer Brand*, Wiley

3 CIPD Employee Outlook, Spring 2015; Hay Group Hearts & Minds Research 2015, www.haygroup.com/en/engaging-minds/; and www.pwc.blogs.com/press_room/2015/04/employee-benefits-preference-varies-according-to-gender-and-age-pwc-research.html

4 Roger D'Aprix (1996), *Communicating for Change*, Wiley

5 Richard Branson (2014), *The Virgin Way*, Virgin Books

6 www.sbaemployerbrand.com

Chapter 4: Direction

1 www.smallbusiness.co.uk/majority-of-small-companies-do-not-last-beyond-five-years-2472867/

2 John Smythe (2007), *The CEO: Chief Engagement Officer: Turning Hierarchy Upside Down to Drive Performance*, Gower

3 www.engageforsuccess.org.uk

4 www.engageforsuccess.org.uk

5 Stephen Covey (1989), *The 7 Habits of Highly Effective People*, Simon & Schuster UK

Chapter 5: Energy

1 www.investopedia.com/articles/investing/060315/top-10-reasons-work-google.asp

2 www.gov.uk/government/uploads/system/uploads/attachment_data/file/366852/PHE_Priorities.pdf

3 www.theguardian.com/small-business-network/2015/aug/28/wellness-workplace-health-initiatives-boost-staff-productivity

4 www.bbc.co.uk/news/blogs-news-from-elsewhere-33805417

5 www.c3health.org/wp-content/uploads/2017/09/Workplace-health-initiatives-review-of-the-evidence-v-2-20140903-1.pdf

6 Lynda Gratton (2011), *The Shift*, Collins

7 www.trainingjournal.com/articles/news/mobile-technology-blame-workplace-stress

8 themindfulnessinitiative.org.uk/images/reports/MI_Building-the-Case_v1.1_Oct16.pdf

9 www.hbr.org/2015/12/why-google-target-and-general-mills-are-investing-in-mindfulness

10 www.pursuit-of-happiness.org/history-of-happiness/mihaly-csikszentmihalyi/

11 Mihaly Csikszentmihalyi (1990), *Flow*, Harper Perennial

12 www.paulareid.com/photos-videos/, and Paula Reid (2016), *Live Life to the Full*, Upfront Publishing

13 www.sloanreview.mit.edu/article/what-creates-energy-in-organizations/

14 www.bain.com/publications/articles/how-leaders-inspire-cracking-the-code.aspx

15 Bernd Vogel and Heike Bruch (2011), *Fully Charged: How Great Leaders Boost Their Organization's Energy and Ignite High Performance*, Harvard Business School Publishing

16 https://sloanreview.mit.edu/article/what-creates-energy-in-organizations/

17 www.bloomberg.com/news/articles/2014-08-29/the-companies-that-can-survive-recession-do-these-things-right

Chapter 6: PRIDE in Practice

1 www.hbr.org/2014/05/from-purpose-to-impact

2 'Business Superbrands Survey 2007' by BMRB and BMRB's sixth 'National Employee Benchmark Study (NEBS)', July 2007

3 www.sdcexec.com/news/10357948/dhl-provides-logistical-support-to-tsunami-hit-countries

4 www.telegraph.co.uk/finance/markets/ftse100/10546379/FTSE-100-at-30-A-big-hand-for-the-Footsie.html

5 www.innosight.com/insight/creative-destruction/

6 www.ted.com/talks/bill_gross_the_single_biggest_reason_why_startups_succeed?utm_campaign=tedspread--b&utm_medium=referral&utm_source=tedcomshare

A Note on the Author

Sheila Parry has worked in business for forty years. For fifteen of them, she ran theblueballroom, a strategic and creative consultancy where she worked with some of the world's largest employers – from adidas to the Deutsche Post DHL Group, Mars Drinks to Siemens – and has developed a deep understanding of how large organisations succeed through getting the best out of people. She is now working as an independent consultant specialising in leadership communications, culture and values, and performance.

Acknowledgements

Writing this book has been a relatively solitary project for me, but I could not have done it without the insights and experience of the hundreds, if not thousands, of people I have observed at work. Firstly, thanks to all those employees in organisations from London to Leeds and Bonn to Beijing who have told their stories and shared their opinions so generously. While none are named in the book, their combined experience of the workplace is the bedrock of the PRIDE model.

I would not have had access to them if it hadn't been for my clients, whether CEOs or project managers, specialists in HR or communications, who allowed me into their organisations. I have thoroughly enjoyed working for them and thank them for their trust.

There are a few individuals who have made important contributions to my thinking as I developed and trialled the concept of PRIDE. These are Dean Capon, Stephen Cheliotis, Chris Chittock, Christina Fee, Ria Hendrikx, Jill Meiburg, Guy Pink and Jack Winters. Special thanks go to Friedrich Georg-Lischke, whose passion for people and work inspired me to dig deeper into what really had to happen to make organisations successful. He was the first person to encourage me to write a book and extraordinarily patient in his support throughout the long process of getting it onto paper.

I would also like to thank all my colleagues and friends who worked alongside me at theblueballroom and gave me the challenge of putting PRIDE into practice. Thanks to them, I have enjoyed some unforgettable moments of pride at work.

Helping me get the book as far as Unbound were Sophie Pentony, Christopher Dean and Catherine Park, and I am grateful for their honest and thorough critique. I have felt in very safe hands ever since with Katy Guest, Georgia Odd and Imogen Denny, who have guided me through the process to publication. Of course the book would not have made it without the advance pledges from my wonderful supporters so thank you to every one of them for having faith in *Take Pride*.

Finally, I would like to mention the constantly enthusiastic support from my family. Hadyn, Mark, David and Robyn, you know only too well how important *Take Pride* is to me and have felt the daily consequences of living with someone who loves their work.

Index

Supporters

Unbound is a new kind of publishing house. Our books are funded directly by readers. This was a very popular idea during the late eighteenth and early nineteenth centuries. Now we have revived it for the internet age. It allows authors to write the books they really want to write and readers to support the books they would most like to see published.

The names listed below are of readers who have pledged their support and made this book happen. If you'd like to join them, visit www.unbound.com.

Denise Allen
Adrian Apthorp
Deborah Aurelius
Brigid Baker
Helen Ballinger
Louise Barrett
Emily Bateman
Sarah Bell
Claire Bose
Suzanne Bourner
Iain Braidwood
Stephanie Brondani
Richard Brooksbank
Alex Butler
Dorota Butler
Clare Campbell
Sara Cannon

Dean Capon
Ezri Carlebach
Simon Carroll
Sheila Carruthers
Penny Clarke
Melanie Cochran
Caroline Cooper
Paul Coubrough
Jean Croft
John Cullinane
Simon Davis
Martin Dixon-Ward
Kate and Phil Douglas
Leona Ellis
Hannah Epps
Felix Escribano
Oliver Facey

Christina Fee
Steve Fenton
Jenni Field
Anna Louise Finn
Bill Fleming
Hilary Galea
Julian Gee
Manjit Ghattaura
Hannah Gray
Jeremy Gray
Anne Groom
Rick Guttridge
Alison Harries
Fiona Head
Joan Hefford
Ria Hendrikx
Elaine Hickmott

James Higginbotham
Liz Hill-Smith
Vanessa Hogge
Institute of Internal
    Communication
Kate Jones
Alex Kearney
Valerie Kemme-
    Smith
Dan Kieran
Lucille Knapp
Gwendy Krijger
Kate Larkin
Petra Limberg
Friedrich Lischke
Ray Longbottom
Katie Macaulay
Micol A. Mancini
Oliver Markham
Katie Marlow
Kevin McDougall
Grainne McKeever
Emily McNeeney
Fiona McNeeney
Matt McNeeney
Emma McNicoll-
    Norbury
Jill Meiburg
Rachel Miller
Kim Mitchell
John Mitchinson
Christine Mockford
Mark Morfett
Gerry Murray
Carlo Navato

Niamh Ni Bheara
Dave Nunn
Hugh O'Neill
Toni O'Sullivan
Richard Oakley
Jacqueline Oldham
David Orr
Jane Paciello
Richard Page
Toby Paice
Catherine Park
Grace Park
Dave Parry
Emma Parry
Hadyn Parry
Mark Parry
Robyn Parry
Advita Patel
Sophie Pentony
Catherine Peters
Clare Phillips
Pivot Consulting Ltd.
Justin Pollard
Nicholas Pow
Siegfried Putzer
Julian Ranger
Jonathan Ratcliff
Charles Reading
Deborah Risby
Margaret Roberts
Michael Roberts
Sarah Roberts
Robyn Roscoe
Heike Saxer-Taylor
Ginnie Scarles

Ian Searle
Euan Semple
M Sue Settell
Andy Shanks
Kate Shanks
Caroline Shearer
Sally Shorthose
Keith Sleight
Philip Smith
Christopher Spokes
Sara Springett
Ralph Stello
Tony Stroud
Hester Thomas
Andrea Thompson
Patricia Thomson
Mairead Turner
Chris Tyler
Ruth Underhill
Tina Vale
Christopher Wade
Sarah Jane Walker
Susan Walker
Christopher Walton
John Ward
Marcus Ward
Dawn Warwick
Jill Wedge
Donie Wiley
Fiona Williams
Jo Winstanley
Jack Winters
Sharmini Woodings
Marc Wright